Special road locomotive, 1890

Steam wagon, 1901

Flexible pantechnicon van, 1924

Overtype 12-ton steam wagon, 1926

6-ton steam wagon, 1928

No. 1 diesel, 1931

Foden type DG6/12 12-ton diesel, 1932

Timber tractor, 1936

Type DG6/15 rigid platform, 1938

THE LONG HAUL

OTHER BOOKS BY MICHAEL SETH-SMITH

Bred for the Purple
Lord Paramount of the Turf
Steve
Two Hundred Years of Richard Johnson & Nephew
History of Steeplechasing
International Stallions and Studs

The assembly of the epicyclic section of a Foden 8-speed gearbox viewed through the epicyclic track gear. *Photographed by Maurice Broomfield.*

Michael Seth-Smith

THE LONG HAUL

*A Social History of the British
Commercial Vehicle Industry*

HUTCHINSON BENHAM, LONDON

HUTCHINSON BENHAM LTD
3 Fitzroy Square, London W1

An imprint of the Hutchinson Group

London Melbourne Sydney Auckland
Wellington Johannesburg and agencies
throughout the world

First published 1975
© Fodens Ltd 1975

Set in Monotype Baskerville

Printed in Great Britain by The Anchor Press Ltd
and bound by Wm Brendon & Son Ltd
both of Tiptree, Essex

ISBN 0 09 124440 4

Contents

List of Illustrations

Frontispiece The assembly of the epicyclic section of a Foden 8-speed gearbox.

Dennis lorry used for breakdown and emergency service
The Pig, Leyland's first petrol-engined vehicle
Foden 5-ton steam wagon, 1910
Leyland lorry, 1910–12
A 1911 28–34 h.p. Halley 3-ton chassis
The Dennis pantechnicon 5-ton chassis, 1911
Commer cars, 1912
R.A.F. Ford lorry, *circa* 1912
R.A.F. Leyland lorry
Box-bodied Foden steamer, 1913
Leyland subsidy-type vehicle, 1914
Dennis, 1913–14
Napier 1-ton, *circa* 1914
Daimler lorry assembly, *circa* 1914

Between pages 56 and 57

Alldays and Onions light trucks, *circa* 1914
Foden steam wagon with 5-ton tipper body and self-loading crane, 1914
Karrier Car, 1914
5-ton Foden steamers, 1914–15
The end of the journey for this crashed Fowler
The popular 7½-cwt Model T Ford van, *circa* 1915
5-ton 'Overtype' steam wagon with tipper body supplied by Fodens to the War Department during the First World War
Five-ton Foden steam wagons line up prior to going into action at the Battle of the Somme
A 1915 Karrier
Foden 5-ton steam wagon, *circa* 1917
Garford, *circa* 1919
Herbert Austin
Leyland G-type, 1920
Leyland, *circa* 1921
Crossley lorries pulling the coffins of victims of the R38 airship tragedy
Leyland overtype tipper of the early 1920s
Several Fodens, 1922

Between pages 88 and 89

1922 Foden bus
Foden D-type 6-ton steam tractor pulling in the Fenland suger beet harvest in the 1920s
Foden 6-ton wagon fitted with showman's equipment, 1923

Halley, mid 1920s

Thornycroft Al six-wheeler, 1926

A forerunner of the Agri-tractor, this steam tractor entered service in 1926

The first P. B. Thornycroft goods lorry in operation at Paddington, 1927

Crossley cross-country car, *circa* 1928

Announced as 'the Thoroughbred British Steam Wagon' this 6-ton Undertype steam wagon was exhibited at the 1928 Commercial Vehicle Show.

A six-wheel pneumatic converted from a 'Super Sentinel' tipping wagon, *circa* 1928

Two Scammell articulated lorries, 1928

Special 1928 D-type Foden steam tractor

Foden E-Undertype six-wheeler steamer of 12 tons, operated probably in the late 1920s

A Speed 12 steam lorry, a Foden demonstration vehicle built in 1929

Foden 6 × 4 E-Undertype steamer with tipper body, 1929

Scammell articulated lorry, 1929

The Morris-Commercial six-wheeler of 1929–30, used in the production of the film *Stampede*

Between pages 104 and 105

Morris-Commercial six-wheeler, 1930

With a 10-ton payload capacity and a 6 × 4 configuration utilizing a double-drive bogie manufactured by Fodens, this vehicle was fitted with a 6LW Gardner engine

A.E.C. Mammoth Major, 1932

An early Foden oiler with 'brown loaf' van body by Beadle, *circa* 1933

A.E.C. plus draw-bar trailer, 1935

When this vehicle appeared in 1934 its design was heralded as years ahead of its time. It was designated the DG4 model

Armstrong Saurer six-wheeler, 1934

Foden 2-ton truck powered by a 3-cylinder Gardner engine, 1935

Ford V8 six-wheeler conversion, 1936

William Foden (1869-1964)

The Foden Motor Works Band, holders of the Crystal Palace Trophy, 1938

Bedford ambulance

Centaur tank manufactured at the Foden works during the Second World War

One of the six prototype 17-lb anti-tank gun towers which were manufactured by Fodens for the British Army during the Second World War

One of the 1750 army trucks supplied by Fodens to the British Army during the Second World War

Scammell 4 × 4 tractor in action at West Watford sub electricity station, 1952

Foreword
by David Foden

The last twenty years have seen great changes in the British motor industry – one of the most significant being the dominance of the commercial vehicle sector. Since the end of the Second World War this sector, once the Cinderella of the motor industry, has become its controlling influence through the strength of those manufacturers now included in the British Leyland Motor Corporation and two companies who still retain their independence – Fodens and E.R.F.

I have been fortunate to have worked in the industry during this period and more fortunate to be associated with Fodens, one of the oldest of the commercial vehicle manufacturers whose history has provided a backcloth of the industry for the past century. That the history of Fodens should be written has been my ambition for many years, but I have always believed that such a history needed to be seen in relation to the saga of the entire industry. A meeting with the publishers, Hutchinson Benham, confirmed my belief, and from this initial discussion the scope of the book was agreed.

Michael Seth-Smith has been writing history and biography for a number of years, particularly in the sphere of horse-racing, and with a successful industrial history behind him, seemed to me to be the obvious choice as the author. He knew little of the motor industry, and less of the commercial vehicle, but as I outlined my thoughts and ideas to him his enthusiasm and interest equalled my own. Since then Michael's intensive research coupled with a genuine fascination for the subject has produced a book which has certainly fulfilled my ambition. I believe that his book will give pleasure not only to those who have an involvement in the industry but to the general reader who I am convinced will find great interest in the history of commercial vehicles as it unfolds against the political, social and industrial scene of the Victorian and Edwardian eras before reaching the years between the two world wars and the present day.

Author's Introduction

No name has greater renown throughout the commercial vehicle industry than Foden, whose directors have sponsored the publication of this book. More than a century ago Edwin Foden hand-built a traction engine in his Sandbach workshop which he sent out to win the Royal Agricultural Society Trials. Today Fodens can produce trucks and dump trucks of the highest quality at the rate of three an hour in their new factory which is amongst the most modern and sophisticated heavy commercial vehicle assembly plants in the world. The history of Fodens and other equally famous manufacturers of commercial vehicles is a vital ingredient, but by no means the only ingredient, in the evolution of the commercial vehicle industry. The ever-changing requirements of operators, the advancement of technical knowledge and engineering skill, the condition of roads throughout the United Kingdom, the antagonism of the railway companies and the apathy of politicians to the needs and demands of the industry are also ingredients of immense importance.

The dawn of the twentieth century saw the establishment of many commercial vehicle companies in the United Kingdom including Albion, Atkinson, Commer, Crossley, Dennis, Foden, Leyland, Maudslay, Morris, Thornycroft and Wolseley. I do not believe that it is possible to divorce their destiny during the past seventy-five years from other vested interests of twentieth-century Britain, against whose backcloth I have attempted to unfold their history. These vested interests often placed obstacles in the path of the youthful industry during its growth to manhood, a growth which began years later than that of the motor industry, although its birth was earlier. A *significant* fact, however, is that, despite a tardy start, the commercial vehicle industry in Britain today both dominates the motor-car industry through the British Leyland Motor Corporation and retains a healthy competition through the independence of Fodens and E.R.F. On a lighter note it should be pointed out that whereas in steamer days a journey could take a day and a firkin of beer, today it can take less than an hour and a cup of tea!

In the autumn of 1973 I was invited to write this social and economic history by David Foden, joint managing director of Fodens, who has given me his friendship for more than twenty years. The original idea for the book was his, and stemmed from his enthusiasm for the industry in which he works. Our initial intention, to which we have adhered, was that the history should concern 'vehicles which deliver goods', and in consequence there is virtually no reference in the text to buses or taxis. Neither are there references to the export aspect of the industry which was considered outside the scope of this book.

As I deepened and widened my researches I became fascinated by the problems and difficulties which the commercial vehicle industry has overcome, and by the initiative shown by the leaders who have guided its destiny. For this reason I have enjoyed my commission which has brought me into contact with many people with immense knowledge of every facet of the industry, based on years of experience. They have generously helped me with advice, information and suggestions and I wish to thank them all – especially Lord Black (a man so distinguished that on his Saturday rounds of golf he had a millionaire as his caddy), who read and criticized my original manuscript; Eric Bellamy, librarian at the National Motor Museum at Beaulieu; the editor of *The Commercial Motor*; A. D. Wilson, secretary of the Lorry Driver of the Year Competition; Ann Hoffman of Author's Research, John Dennis (my brother-in-law), Richard Seth-Smith of British Leyland Truck and Bus Division, the publicity officers of many commercial vehicle manufacturers, and finally everyone at Fodens' Elworth Works who patiently answered a multitude of my questions.

Sylvans,
Farnham, Surrey
May 1975

I

In Lewis Carroll's famous Victorian classic *Alice in Wonderland* the King decrees: 'Begin at the beginning, and go on until you come to the end; then stop.' His command is supremely logical but raises the intriguing problem of deciding the moment when the beginning commences. The words 'Once upon a time' which have been used on countless occasions to excuse the absence of precise origins lost in antiquity are not sufficient. A history must be more explicit, and if the King's decree is to be heeded an exact date should be established for the beginning of the history of the commercial vehicle industry in Britain. This date was 14th November 1896 when the new Locomotives on Highways Act came into force.

The year 1896 found Great Britain at the zenith of her prosperity and prestige. Britannia ruled the waves, her Empire stretched to the farthest corners of the world, and she had become the greatest Imperial power in the history of the world. The dreams of the Colonial Secretary, Joseph Chamberlain, for territorial expansion were matching the ambitions of Cecil Rhodes to secure British sovereignty over the entire African continent from the Cape to Tanganyika, whilst Rudyard Kipling, with his patriotic jingles, was capturing the imagination of the British public in an era when there were no cinema idols or television stars upon whom to lavish hero worship. Kipling's creed that leadership was the right and duty of the white man – especially the Anglo-Saxon — gratified the egoism of a nation which rejoiced that the sun never set upon the Empire of its Queen who was to celebrate her Diamond Jubilee the next summer.

Three years earlier the Independent Labour Party had been founded, and the Fabian Society issued its manifesto suggesting the ownership by the community of the means of production, distribution and exchange. It was a revolutionary suggestion at a time when the winds of change, influenced by the approaching dawn of a new century, were bringing drastic ideas and concepts of society. Bernard Shaw, a member of the Fabian Society, was beginning to shock theatre audiences by the outspokenness of his plays, whilst Ibsen's *A Doll's House* was giving a clue to the future emancipation of women. The word 'emancipation' was on everyone's lips, especially of those women who were smoking cigarettes in public, playing out-door games and adopting the new vogue of separate blouses and skirts – skirts which were becoming shorter as thick petticoats became unfashionable. Gentlemen were also contemplating greater casualness in their attire, with lounge suits and bowler hats replacing frock-coats and top hats, whilst artisans and clerks were finding that the influx of inexpensive ready-made clothes suited both their requirements and their pockets. The sewing machine, cheap soap, matches and paraffin were aiding the home comforts of those of limited resources, many of whom were having more leisure in consequence of the introduction of the shorter working day. More leisure was causing a reawakening to the beauties of the English countryside – a reawakening stimulated by the founding of the National Trust – and bicycling was becoming the popular weekend pastime of those who sang

> It won't be a stylish marriage
> I can't afford a carriage
> But you'll look sweet upon the seat
> Of a bicycle made for two

as they pedalled away from the drabness of industrial cities and towns to discover a freedom and paradise on roads uncluttered by other forms of transport. The craze for bicycles had caused many small engineering firms, particularly in the Midlands, to manufacture bicycle components. By 1879 there were more than sixty such firms, the best known of which were Rudge of Wolverhampton and Humber of Nottingham. Six years later the original 'safety' bicycle was built by J. K. Starley of Coventry. Mr E. Oxborrow became the first man to bicycle from Land's End to John o' Groats, and cyclists were no longer referred to as 'elephants on casters'. The enthusiasm for bicycling led to the formation in 1878 of the Cyclists' Touring Club which eventually found the financial resources for the establishment of the Roads Improvement Association. When the Automobile Association was formed a decade later a powerful pressure group came into existence to call attention to their present grievances and future hopes concerning the condition of the roads. Further progress was made by the introduction of the pneumatic tyre patented by John Boyd Dunlop, a Scottish veterinary surgeon who lived in Belfast. The result of his experiments, carried out with materials bought from a local chemist's shop, in order to overcome the discomfort suffered by his young son who rode a tricycle fitted with a solid rubber tyre, made the bicycle an even more popular form of transport. Nevertheless letters, under the heading 'Tyranny of the Road', appeared in *The Times* complaining of the dangerous and excessive speeds of cyclists – even though the roads that they used were almost deserted. In the latter half of the nineteenth century the only users of the roads were local travellers, short-haul carriers, farmers taking their livestock to market and the cyclists, for the advent of the railways in Victorian England had resulted in both goods and passengers being transported long distances by rail. The railway companies had not found their initial task easy, for they were opposed by the bigotry of those who took a pride in being reactionaries to progress. Landowners claimed that the railways would ruin their estates, whilst canal, turnpike and coach proprietors clamoured that the railways would cause them to become bankrupt. In the midst of the outcry a Press campaign was started to emphasize that the railways would make cows too frightened to yield milk, that smoke from the funnels of the engines would kill birds, and sparks would set fire to the roofs of houses. It needed the success of the Stockton–Darlington railway to convince the public that the future of the railways was limitless. Such a realization sounded the death-knell for road improvement for fifty years, for the preoccupation with the building of more and more railway lines strangled all incentive for the maintenance of existing roads, even though some of the railway proposals were preposterous. They were so far-fetched that the magazine *Punch* could not resist suggesting 'A Great North Pole Railway forming a junction with the Equinoctial Line with a branch to the Horizon'.

Another reason for the decline in any interest for the future development of roads was the excessive tolls on turnpikes and the equally excessive and short-sighted legislation banning from roads all but the heaviest agricultural engines. Gone for ever were the days of the mail-coach so vividly described by George Eliot: '. . . Five and thirty years ago the glory had not yet departed from the old coaching roads. The great roadside inns were still brilliant with well-polished tankards, the smiling glances of pretty barmaids, and the repartee of jocose ostlers. The mail still announced itself by the merry note of the horn, and the hedgecutter or the rick thatcher might still know the exact hour by the unfailing yet otherwise meteoric apparition of the pea-green Tally Ho or the yellow independent.' The short-sighted legislation which contributed to the deterioration of the highways resulted from the total lack of imagination on the part of successive governments to the importance of road transport.

Nothing could have been a greater set-back than the notorious and crippling 'Red Flag' Acts of 1861 and 1865 which imposed speed limits of 4 m.p.h. in open country and 2 m.p.h. in towns. The Acts, passed in the closing years of Lord Palmerston's Ministry, required that all 'road locomotives' be attended by at least three people, one of whom was to walk sixty yards ahead of the engine with a red flag by day and a red lantern by night. The Acts were ones of pure folly and illustrated the incompetence and disinterest of those in authority who instigated them. They strangled the incentive of engineers and designers, and effectively clamped down on road improvements. Not until 1888, when the Local Government Act set up County Councils, was there a reassessment of the situation, although the Public Health Act of 1872, which transferred the authority of the Home Office over highways and turnpike roads to that of the Local Government Board, was a step in the right direction. During the early 1890s so many pressures were building up that it became obvious that a safety valve would have to be opened to unleash the pent-up energies of those eager to drive motor vehicles at reasonable speeds upon adequate roads. The momentous step to open the safety valve was taken in the year 1896, when Henry Chaplin, President of the Local Government Board, and a member of Lord Salisbury's Cabinet, introduced a Bill into the House of Commons to make possible the use of 'light locomotives' on public roads.

Henry Chaplin, fifty-five years of age and the personal friend of the Prince of Wales since the days when they had been undergraduates at Oxford, had been the innocent party in the Society scandal of 1864 when his fiancée, Lady Florence Paget, had eloped with the profligate and dissolute Marquess of Hastings only a few days before the wedding. At the age of twenty-five Chaplin had become Master of the Burton Hounds and entered Parliament as Conservative Member for mid-Lincolnshire. Hunting was the love of his life and he once remarked, 'I often think that Providence intended me to be a huntsman and not a statesman.' In 1889 he had been appointed President of the Board of Agriculture with Cabinet rank, and was a member of the Royal Commission set up to enquire into the parlous state of agriculture and the economic depression caused by foreign competition. At heart a countryman, Chaplin thought that

20

the new Locomotives Bill might be another nail in the coffin of landowners and farmers. The Lincolnshire farmers were his friends and he knew that they were afraid of the revolution caused by the advent of so many new forms of mechanization. He also knew that they trusted him, not merely because he travelled around his constituency regaling all and sundry from hampers containing mountains of food and Pommery '74, but also because he was a 'sporting squire'. It was understandable that he was in a quandary in introducing the Bill, for he had divided loyalty. However, he was fair-minded enough to discuss it with one of the pioneers of motoring, Sir David Salomons, who had organized the first public motor exhibition in Britain on 15th October 1895. The exhibition, held in Tunbridge Wells where Salomons was mayor, attracted only six entries, three of which were French. Nevertheless, encouraged by the interest shown in the exhibition, Salomons founded the Liverpool Self Propelled Traffic Association, and in the first months of 1896 led a deputation from the association to see Chaplin. For the next few months as the Bill was being drafted Salomons was asked his opinion on various of its proposed clauses. It was made clear to him, however, that the views of highway authorities were to be considered, and that their opinions and preferences would carry more weight than those of the newly formed motoring organizations. During the summer the Motor Car Club was founded – a society for the protection, encouragement and development of the motor car and horseless-carriage industry – and held shows and competitions in London, announcing that once the Bill was passed, the club proposed to 'develop its social side upon the lines of the Automobile Club of Paris'. The enthusiasm of the club was not shared by everyone, even though recognition to the motor car was given by the Prince of Wales having his first drive, and the *Daily Mail* carried an editorial which stated: '. . . the motor carriage will never displace the smart trotting horse or the high stepping team, but it will end the cruel labours of the poor equine drudges that strain before omnibus and dray, and save the broken down favourite of the Turf from the bondage of the nocturnal cab'.

When Henry Chaplin, broad-shouldered and wearing a monocle, outlined the Locomotives Bill in June he explained that considerable spadework on the Bill had been completed by the previous government of the Liberal leader Lord Rosebery. First mention of the Bill had been on 14th February when Lord Harris asked for the first Reading. He said that the object was to exempt light locomotives from certain statutory measures and then to impose restrictions on weight and traction. Lord Clifden asked if the Bill contemplated electricity as a motive power, and Lord Harris replied that it did not exclude it. There were no other speakers on the Bill which was presented and read. On 19th May the Lords sat in committee on the Bill, with the Earl of Morley in the chair. Various amendments were discussed and agreed re weight, the definition of light locomotive, fines for breach of regulations, penalties for negligent driving, and the Bill's application to Scotland and Ireland. On 16th June the Bill was passed and sent to the Commons.

Curiously there are no detailed reports of the first Reading in the House of Commons three days later. When Mr Chaplin moved the second Reading, however, he prophesied that '. . . the Bill would undoubtedly develop a very great, and having regard to the experience with bicycles, quite possibly an enormous trade and give a vast amount of employment . . . it was even possible that these motor cars might become a rival to light railways . . . and would help farmers transport their products . . .'. One member of the Opposition, Dr Tanner from Co. Cork, spoke volubly against the Bill and stated that '. . . the Hon. gentleman was introducing a Bill for the popularizing of machines which were antagonistic to horseflesh and therefore to genuine sport . . .'. Other speakers included the First Lord of the Treasury, but it was left to a far-sighted backbencher to claim '. . . we should give the Bill a fair chance for in the future there must be a vast industry in auto-motor cars. . . '. Further amendments to the Bill were made in committee stage, including requirements that light locomotives should carry lights at night. The most important alteration to previous Highways Acts was the repeal of the ludicrous impositions of the 'Red Flag' Act by the raising of the speed limit to 14 m.p.h. Other clauses of the Act stated that motorists were not to cause their vehicles to travel backwards for a greater distance or time than may be required for safety; to keep to the left when meeting any carriage or horse, and to the right when overtaking them; not to obstruct the highway; and on the request of any police constable, or of any person having charge of a restive horse, or for that purpose, cause the light locomotive to stop and remain stationary so long as may be reasonably necessary.

Shortly after the Act received the Royal Assent on 14th August, Sir David Salomons wrote to the Press:

It behoves everyone concerned to act with prudence and consideration, to do nothing which might injure the roads, to use every care not to frighten horses, nor to store dangerous liquids thoughtlessly . . . but to act with discretion so that it shall not be said in a year or two hence that the freedom now given had been too great, and that another Act must be demanded to control the reprehensible conduct of those who may misuse their privileges. . . .

The first outward and visible sign of the significance of the Act was the organizing by Harry J. Lawson, one of the first entrepreneurs of the motor industry, of the Emancipation Run to Brighton. It had been Lawson's intention to hold the run in October, but as a result of police refusal to allow the event before the passing of the new Act, the run was postponed for a month. This refusal indicated that the police in general, and the Metropolitan Police in particular, were not prepared to give concessions to motorists. The fur-coated, goggled motorist, wearing his cap back to front, became the target of good-natured banter in the music halls and jokes about him appeared in *Punch*, with illustrations of policemen hiding in hedge-rows armed with stop-watches. It became evident that the police, following the beliefs of politicians, did not envisage the highways of Britain being congested with privately owned motor cars. Even more evident was the realization that no one contemplated the crowding of the roads with commercial vehicles to be a remote possibility.

The evolution of the commercial vehicle industry, which followed in the wake of the evolution of the private motor car, is inseparably linked with the development of the roads. Although Watling Street, Ermine Street and the Fosse Way were constructed by the Romans during their occupation of Britain, little was done to prevent such major roads from falling into disrepair once the legions of Caesar departed. It was not until an Act of Parliament in 1555 which com-pelled parishes to build and maintain roads that the situation im-proved. The introduction of turnpike roads towards the end of the seventeenth century improved the situation still further.

Years later the resourcefulness of men such as John Metcalf, Thomas Telford and John MacAdam resulted in the quality of the road surface benefitting to a greater extent. Metcalf, 'Blind Jack of Knaresborough', had lost his sight as a child of six after contracting smallpox. Despite this handicap, he became a man of incredible determination. At the age of twenty-two he learned that his sweet-heart was to be married to another – eloped with her on the eve of the wedding and married her the next day. He died at the age of ninety-three, leaving more than ninety great-grandchildren and a reputation as the outstanding road-builder of his era.

MacAdam had been appointed General Surveyor of Roads to the Bristol Turnpike Trust in 1816. Within a year of this appointment the Post Office Authorities in London became aware of the fact that the Bristol to London coach made extraordinarily good time at the Bristol end of the journey. Enquiries elucidated the fact that this increased speed was due to the roads of MacAdam. The matter was brought to the notice of one of the two Postmasters General, Lord Chichester, who asked MacAdam to improve the roads in East Sussex and in particular the Brighton to Lewes road. In return Lord

Chichester helped and advised MacAdam in the difficult task of persuading His Majesty's Government to recompense him for the costly experiments that he had made at his own expense over the years. MacAdam wanted £6857 3s. 6d. and the Treasury eventually paid the sum in full – including the 3s. 6d. MacAdam, who has been wittily described as 'The Colossus of Roads', had originally published his findings in an essay in 1819 after having practised and perfected a system of road-making in Ayrshire. In addition to his expenses being returned to him, the Treasury made him grants which totalled almost £10000.

During the years of the pioneer road-builders when the glory and romance of the mail-coach was at its peak, engineers of vision and enterprise on both sides of the English Channel were steadfastly persevering in their efforts to build horseless carriages. French artillery officer Joseph Cugnot was imprisoned after his horseless carriage had overturned in the streets of Paris in 1769, and Richard Trevithick designed and built a steam carriage which transported passengers from Paddington to Leather Lane in 1803. Having inspected Trevithick's machine, Sir Humphrey Davy wrote to a friend: 'I shall soon hope to hear that the roads of England are the haunts of Captain Trevithick's dragons.' It was the general consensus of opinion that such machines might prove useful for the transport of passengers, although the thought that they might be used with equal success to carry goods was beyond the imagination and comprehension of all but a few visionaries.

It was not until the end of the Napoleonic Wars that steam-driven vehicles made their presence felt on the roads of Britain. Although their appearance was greeted with horror by many of the dashing cavalry officers who had fought in the Peninsular Campaign and at Waterloo, the new machines met with general approval – approval which was endorsed when the Duke of Wellington dared to travel on one of the first steam carriages built by Goldsworth Gurney. His example encouraged those of lesser bravado. When Gurney's first steam coach was journeying from London to Bath, however, its passengers were stoned by irate ostlers who visualized the coach as a menace to their livelihood. During the first half of Queen Victoria's reign the Crimean War and the Indian Mutiny were fought, Penny Postage was introduced, Darwin published his *Origin of Species*, and the advancement of engineering and science grew apace, with the inventions of Marconi, Edison, Faraday and Bell giving the world new concepts of sound and light. In 1834 the first fatal accident to passengers of a mechanically propelled vehicle had occurred when John Scott Russell's coach boiler exploded on a road near Paisley, killing five people. Such disasters were ammunition for the antagon-

The Smithy in Water Street, Leyland, where the foundations of the present undertaking were laid

FOUNDED IN 1896

It is difficult to realise that from a small rural forge has sprung the vast organisation now known as Leyland Motors, Ltd., yet such is the case.

As early as 1885 experiments for utilising steam-power for driving road wagons were being carried out, with no little success in a blacksmith's shop in Leyland, but it was not until after the passing of the Locomotives on the Highways Act in 1896 that these experiments were brought to a successful conclusion by a Company styled The Lancashire Steam Motor Company, which was formed in that year. This Company was the forerunner of the present world-wide organisation. It acquired small works in Herbert Street, Leyland, and its first steam wagon was built in 1897. This vehicle secured the first prize at Trials organised by the Royal Agricultural Society in 1897.

The Herbert Street Works, a small factory that served early Leyland purposes in 1896

An early account of Leyland beginnings

Left They liked a good load in 1897. This Leyland, a 3-ton steamer, was the first of its model sold. Fox Bros & Co. Ltd of Wellington, Somerset, were the owners. *British Leyland*

Right Lawrence Gardner, founder of L. Gardner & Sons Ltd, 1868. *Gardner Engines Ltd*

Below left Gottlieb Daimler (*right*) and his closest collaborator Wilhelm Maybach (*second right*) introduced this 5-ton truck with a two-cylinder Phoenix engine at the automobile exhibition in Paris in June 1898. *Mercedes Benz*

Below The original staff, with apprentices, of Leyland's Herbert Street works, James Sumner is on the left and Henry Spurrier on the right. *British Leyland*

This 4-ton Foden steam wagon was operated as a brewer's wagon. It first entered service in 1900 and was reconstructed in March 1907

1901 Belle. *National Motor Museum, Beaulieu*

Fodens' brass band was born on Mafeking night. This photograph was taken in 1904 and shows all the original members of the band. William Foden, son of the founder Edwin Foden, was the euphonium player (*third from right*)

A 1904 De Dion Bouton motor car with Mr E. R. Foden, later founder of the other Sandbach-based lorry company, at the wheel

The first steam wagon leaves the Leyland works, with Henry Spurrier the Second at the tiller. *British Layland*

The Borough of Chelsea were keen users of Leyland steamers from the first. They amassed this impressive fleet between 1900 and 1906. *British Leyland*

The machine shop at Barton Hall Engine Works of L. Gardner & Sons Ltd, Patricroft, *circa* 1908. *Gardner Engines Ltd*

Country house car by Dennis, *circa* 1908. The large areas of glass suggest station work rather than the butts or the moors, as does the large luggage rack. Note the dual solids at the rear. *National Motor Museum, Beaulieu*

Left Edwin Foden (1841–1911), founder of Fodens Ltd.

Below left Dr. Rudolf Diesel (1858–1913). *Radio Times Hulton Picture Library*

Below right The Rt Hon. Henry Chaplin, M.P. (1841–1923). *Radio Times Hulton Picture Library*

ists of steam carriages, who found a champion and an advocate in the poet William Morris, who wrote:

Forget six counties overhung with smoke
Forget the snorting steam and piston stroke
Forget the spreading of the hideous town
Think rather of the pack horse on the Down.

The invention which finally routed the reactionaries, and at the same time challenged the supremacy of the steam engine and the railways, was the gas engine of Jean-Joseph Etienne Lenoir, who in 1860 had invented the sparking plug and devised the tremble coil ignition. Almost a hundred years earlier Alessandro Volta had ignited explosive gases with an electric spark, whilst in 1820 William Cecil discovered the principle of ignition for gas engines. The internal combustion engine presented immense advantages, for not only was it simple in principle, but the lightness in weight and the smallness in size by comparison to steam boilers enabled greater scope to designers. One of those who heard of the success of Lenoir's invention was a twenty-nine-year-old engineer, Nicolaus Otto, who lived in Cologne. Otto experimented for almost twenty years before perfecting his four-stroke engine and establishing a factory for manufacturing gas engines at Deutz near Cologne. Whilst Otto was experimenting and designing in Germany, men such as Count de Dion, M. Bouton, A. Bollée and Léon Serpollet were proving their pioneering genius in France. None of them, however, was the equal of Gottlieb Daimler, who was for a time Otto's manager at Deutz. Daimler, born in 1844, and ultimately acknowledged as the greatest pioneer of the motor industry in Europe, resigned from the Gasmorten Fabrik Deutz in 1882, and established his own works at Cannstat where he persuaded Wilhelm Maybach, one of Otto's designers, to join him. Twelve months later Daimler introduced his hot-tube ignition which became the forerunner of Robert Bosch's low-tension magneto. Initially, after setting up on his own, Daimler concentrated upon building engines for bicycles and tricycles and did not complete his first four-wheeled car until 1886. Meanwhile Karl Benz, a man fourteen years younger than Daimler, was carrying out further experiments at Mannheim and building petrol engines for motor vehicles which proved so successful that by 1890 Emile Roger had taken out licences under patent to sell Roger-Benz cars in France. Daimler patents were also taken out in France by Emile Levassor, who had begun to supply Panhard et Levassor cars on a commercial basis. With no restrictions to confine their activities on the highway the French and German designers, inventors and manufacturers far outpaced their British rivals in the formative years of the motor industry. Road races and competitions were held, testing the speed and endurance of the machines on runs from Paris to Rouen, and Paris to Bordeaux, whilst in England until 1888 a man still was compelled by law to precede motor vehicles with a red flag (although the size of this was not stipulated). Despite this farcical state of affairs, some Englishmen were prepared to consider the future. The Crossley brothers had acquired the world rights (excluding Germany) of some of Otto's patents and in 1895 John Henry Knight, who had made several trips to Paris and was the friend of the leading French manufacturers, produced a 2¾ h.p. single-cylinder-engined motor car at his Farnham workshop. In the same year Frederick Lanchester exhibited his first car. Sadly, however, few of those affluent enough to buy British vehicles were convinced of their efficiency. The Hon. C. S. Rolls ordered an 8 h.p. four-cylinder Panhard et Levassor, and another motorist, having collected a French-built car at Southampton Docks, drove it home – a distance of seventy miles – in bottom gear as the instruction handbook was printed in French and he could not interpret it! The roads from Southampton along which the unfortunate motorist drove were typical of the era, for they were dusty, uneven and pitted with holes. So little interest had been taken in road maintenance since the monopoly of the railways that such a condition was inevitable. It was a hazard reluctantly accepted by all those who envisaged both motor cars and commercial vehicles using the Queen's Highway.

In 1860, the year that Lenoir invented his gas engine, a nineteen-year-old Cheshire boy, Edwin Foden, was appointed foreman at Messrs Plant and Hancock's engineering works at Elworth, near Sandbach. The son of a shoemaker in the local village of Smallwood, Edwin had left school at an early age to begin his working life as the village post boy. Every spare moment of his leisure hours found him industriously creating model steam engines from cocoa tins, odd bits of metal and wire. Obsessed by engineering, he persuaded his father to allow him to be apprenticed at Plant and Hancocks on his fifteenth birthday. Four years later, although delighted by his promotion to foreman, he left the works to gain greater experience in the railway engine works at Crewe, and subsequently in a factory at Kidsgrove. Throughout this period he never lost contact with Mr Hancock, who considered him the brightest and cleverest young man whom he had ever employed. In 1866 Hancock decided to retire and offered Edwin Foden the chance to take control of the business. One of the most famous commercial vehicle manufacturers in the world was established as a result of Edwin Foden accepting Mr Hancock's offer.

For the next decade Edwin Foden concentrated upon improving the type of agricultural machinery and portable steam engines which had been produced by Plant and Hancock. In the North-West of England the firm's products had acquired an enviable reputation for workmanship, design and reliability, and the report of the Royal Agricultural Society of England for 1883 it was stated: '. . . Mr Foden's invention seems to be of great merit in simplifying without lessening efficiency. That a machine so constructed may be made for considerably less cost is evident from the reduction of working parts. Equally apparent is the considerable saving in power in driving a machine in which the gear is so much simplified. The catalogue price of the machine is £165. . . .'

To Edwin Foden, ambitious and enterprising, the sales horizons offered by these products were not sufficiently wide, particularly now that his sixteen-year-old-son William had joined the firm after leaving Sandbach Grammar School and receiving a thorough grounding in the technique of marketing and management. Edwin determined that in future he would turn his attention to the manufacture of traction engines. Critical of his own efforts, he continually modified and tested his prototype before he was prepared to offer his first traction engine for sale. In 1887, the year after Gottlieb Daimler produced his first car, and William Foden's name appeared as a Director of Fodens for the first time, Edwin Foden won the Royal Agricultural Society's Trials at Newcastle with a compound traction engine operating at a pressure of 250 lb, and with a fuel consumption of only 1·84 lb per brake horse-power per hour. Sales began to increase rapidly, and grateful customers wrote in praise of their Foden vehicles: 'I beg to state that I have driven engines made by several others and I can candidly say yours beats them all, she is the talk of the town.'

Three years earlier, after a Foden traction engine had won the Stockport Traction Engine Trials, organized by the Royal Agricultural Society, an article appeared in the magazine *The Engineer* suggesting that some of the tractor manufacturing companies, which were larger than Fodens, should look to their laurels unless they were prepared to be superseded by the tractors built at the Elworth works.

In the last years of the century Edwin Foden appreciated that transport could not possibly be prevented by existing Highway Acts and restrictive laws from increasing its use of the roads. Although his traction engines were becoming faster, more efficient and able to haul heavier loads, he was sufficiently far-sighted to realize that the steam wagon must have a greater future than any traction locomotive. A pioneer of the commercial vehicle industry, he began to develop the prototype of a steam wagon which would prove itself to be better in every respect than any other comparable machine on the market.

John Thornycroft was another pioneer who was experimenting

with steam locomotives, and by 1896 had produced a van of one-ton capacity, which he described as 'a very harmless-looking vehicle as it shows no funnel or machinery, and is really quite silent'. Despite Thornycroft's description, when the locomotive first arrived in Kensington High Street a horse in a van some distance away proceeded to try to climb up a lamp-post in his terrified efforts to avoid the monster! Later in the year a note in the *Westminster Gazette* stated: 'Much excitement was caused at Windsor by the advent of the Thornycroft steam van which proceeded up Thames Street to Castle Hill. The motor greatly interested onlookers and was followed by a number of spectators to the Datchet Road where it stopped for a time. The carriage is available for goods, parcels and passengers and carries a ton. No smoke or steam is visible and there is no smell.'

Firms were beginning to take an interest in such vehicles, and in 1897 Carter Paterson ordered their first motor van – a chain-driven Daimler of 10 cwt capacity – which ran between the West End of London and the City for six months before being destroyed in a fire at Carter Paterson's Goswell Road warehouse.

Meanwhile the War Office was having thoughts about the future of mechanized vehicles as a form of transport for the Army. Kitchener's campaign to reconquer the Sudan, and the disastrous failure of the British forces in South Africa at the commencement of the Boer War, had stirred up considerable agitation amongst Britain's military leaders. The 'Khaki' Election in October 1900, coming at a time when patriotism was high due to the tide of war turning in Britain's favour and Lord Roberts' occupation of Johannesburg, made the Government wake up to the probability of mechanized warfare in the future. Almost fifty years earlier James Boydell's steam tractor had dragged heavy loads in the Crimea when the Allied armies were besieging Sebastopol, but had proved unsatisfactory. From time to time during the later years of the nineteenth century inventors had forwarded plans and specifications for fighting vehicles to the War Office, but they had been discarded as the futuristic notions of eccentrics and crack-pots. The dawn of the twentieth century, the death of Queen Victoria, and news that both the French and German High Commands were interested in strengthening their military forces with mechanical transport prodded the War Office into action. In December 1901 the War Office Committee on Mechanical Transport, of which the Right Honourable Arthur Stanley, M.P., was president, and whose members included an 'Associate member for India' held a competition for self-propelled lorries for military purposes. A first prize of £500, a second prize of £250 and a third prize of £100 were offered by the Secretary of State for War. In the competition notes it was made a condition that 'His Majesty's

Government' have the right to purchasing after the trials any or all of the competing vehicles at the price stated by the competitors. The listed requirements of the self-propelled lorry included:

(i) The lorry to be used upon rough roads, or to a limited extent across country. To be able to go wherever a country cart can go.
(ii) The lorry to be able to run for 48 hours without overhaul or cleaning.
(iii) The lorry, carrying its full net load of 3 tons, and drawing a trailer loaded with 2 tons, to be capable
  (a) of a speed of 8 m.p.h. on fairly level roads in fair conditions.
  (b) of a mean speed of at least 5 m.p.h. on average roads, up and down hill.
  (c) of taking its full load without assistance on an average road up and down a slope of 1 in 8.

At the end of the competition notes was an additional note: In considering the merits of the competing vehicles, special importance will be paid to the following points:

(a) Price having regard to efficiency.
(b) Distance that can be travelled by the vehicles when fully loaded with 5 tons, with the fuel and water carried on the lorry. (Great importance will be attached to this.)
(c) Economy in weight.
(d) Durability.
(e) Accessibility of all parts.
(f) Simplicity of design.
(g) Ease of manipulation.
(h) Absence of noise, vibration and smoke.

A further condition was that a 'detention' allowance of five shillings a day would be paid by the Secretary of State for War to one attendant for each vehicle for every day during the period of the trials. An especial warning was given that 'on no account are competing vehicles to pass each other when descending steep hills, nor when crossing bridges'. The trials, which lasted for seventeen days, included a thirty-mile route from Aldershot via Odiham, Bagshot and Farnborough before returning to Aldershot, and a thirty-four-mile route via Guildford, Farnham and Worplesdon. Eleven firms, including Thornycroft's Steam Wagon Co. and Fodens, entered for the trials with Fodens winning the first prize. On 10th December the *Daily Chronicle* had reported: '. . . The steam wagon by Foden and Co. came in first – for the third successive time. A long hill between two and three miles in length between Odiham and Alton, over a very poor by-road, tested the capabilities of the types severely – but the Foden seemed to make light of the work. . . .' Six weeks later in the *Daily Express* a correspondent wrote: '. . . The decided superiority of the Foden wagon soon became manifest – day by day the sturdy little vehicle came through the trying tests ahead of the other wagons and showing consistently superior economy in working, consuming far less coal and water than any of the other competitors. . . .' When the trials were over the judges issued their report. In it they stated:

. . . the trials at Aldershot have shown that these steam lorries are good and serviceable machines suitable for present supply, and likely to be of great advantage to the transport service in countries where fuel and water in sufficient quantity is available . . . compared with horse draught, these Trials have shown that self-propelled lorries can transport 5 tons of stores at about 6 m.p.h. over very considerable distances on hilly average British roads under winter conditions. The load transported by each lorry (5 tons) if carried in horse wagons of service pattern, would overload three G.S. wagons, requiring twelve draught horses besides riding horses, whose pace would not ordinarily exceed 3 m.p.h. Moreover the marching of 197 miles in six consecutive days over hilly roads would not have been accomplished by horses even at that speed without the assistance of spare horses.

At the same time that the trials were taking place Frederick R. Simms was inventing the first armoured car powered by an internal combustion engine. Simms, a brilliant and versatile engineer, had been responsible for importing the first Daimler car into England. During a visit to Bremen in the late autumn of 1880 Simms had seen a motor tramcar built by Daimler. Believing that the tramcar had commercial prospects in England, he persuaded Gottlieb Daimler to allow him to take over all the Daimler patents for the United Kingdom and the colonies, except for Canada. A friendship was struck up between Simms and Daimler, and Simms became a director of the German Daimler Company. In 1893 Simms formed a private company, the Daimler Motor Syndicate Limited, in London which took over the business of Simms and Company and ostensibly had the intention of fitting Daimler engines into motor boats. The new company was hardly launched when Harry J. Lawson, together with Terence Hooley, bought the agency and manufacturing rights from Simms and established the Daimler Motor Company. Lawson was shrewd, enterprising and determined to gain a monopoly of the motor industry by a series of financial deals at a time when the law concerning company accounts left much to be desired by modern standards. He was far too astute for many of the engineers, manufacturers and designers whom he bamboozled by a host of share transactions from one grandiose sounding company to another. The only people who did not suffer were those unimpressed by his showmanship and exuberance.

Meanwhile, Simms was experimenting with 'war machines', and

built four-wheeled motor cycles armed with a single Maxim machine gun – a gun first exhibited by Hiram Maxim in 1884. Maxim, a naturalized British subject, had been born in Maine, U.S.A., in 1840 and arrived in England in 1881. A man of affluence, he established a workshop in Hatton Garden where he began experimenting with firearms and evolved the machine gun which bears his name. Simms decided to create a larger and more powerful machine which was built as a joint venture by Vickers and Maxim. The new machine was an indication that the European arms race had begun, and that Britain, Germany and France were all aware that strength of arms on land and sea could lead to further territorial aggrandisement.

Whilst Edwin Foden was laying the foundations of his successful business at Sandbach, another pioneer, John Cawsy Dennis, was opening a bicycle shop in Guildford, Surrey. John Dennis, born in 1871, was the middle son of a Devonshire farmer. It was accepted that his elder brother would eventually inherit the family farm, and in consequence John Dennis was apprenticed to the owner of an ironmongery business in nearby Bideford. He enjoyed his work, showed an aptitude for any task requiring mechanical skill, and was fascinated by the details of bicycles that he read in trade catalogues. One of the firms that sold bicycles was Filmer and Mason in Guildford. Requiring more fitters for the components that they bought, they put advertisements in the trade magazines. John Dennis read one of these advertisements, applied for the job, and was accepted. For the next few years he worked in Guildford, spent a further eighteen months in London learning more details of the trade when in the employment of Brown Bros who were engineering factors, and gradually acquired the confidence in his own ability so necessary for anyone planning to establish his own business. Fired with enthusiasm and convinced that he could buy bicycle components direct from manufacturers, assemble them and sell them at a profit, he returned to Guildford in the autumn of 1894. Soon after New Year's Day he opened his shop at No. 94 High Street to which he gave the rather grandiloquent title of the Universal Athletic Stores. At the rear of the premises was a backyard where the bicycle components were assembled with the frames suspended by a rope from an old pear tree. On 'Opening Day' John Dennis attracted crowds by staging a wheel-spinning competition in the window of the shop. At 7 p.m. the captain of the Guildford Cycling Club started the front wheel of a bicycle spinning whilst onlookers were invited to guess how long it would revolve. At the end of twelve minutes and ten seconds the wheel came to rest, thereby winning first prize of a Lucas cycle lamp for a woman who had correctly estimated the duration of the spin. Until Joseph Lucas had introduced an oil lamp to fit the hub of penny farthings in 1878, and had steadily improved the efficiency of his lamps ever since, there had been considerable difficulty in providing suitable lights for all types of vehicles.

Within months of opening his shop John Dennis found that trade was so brisk that he invited his younger brother Raymond to join him, to act as general assistant and to pay particular attention to increasing sales. Raymond Dennis spent his evenings teaching Guildford residents how to ride a bicycle, either along the lanes leading to the Hog's Back in summer, or in a local drill hall in winter. Once taught, the enthusiasts would buy either 'The Speed King' or 'The Speed Queen', both assembled beneath the old pear tree. During the Jubilee celebrations of 1897 there was a procession of horse-drawn floats through the streets of Guildford. John Dennis entered a float of which the centre-piece was a ten-foot-high bicycle with a scarlet-clad Mephistopheles in the saddle. Much to the delight of the two Dennis brothers their float was awarded first prize.

Before the end of the nineteenth century John Dennis had changed from merely assembling bicycle components to manufacturing them. He exhibited at the Crystal Palace Show, and offered a 'Popular' model for eleven guineas and a 'Roadster' for sixteen guineas. The old pear tree was cut down and the backyard converted into an additional workshop where a 6 h.p. Crossley gas engine was installed, together with a plating vat, enamelling stoves and other new plant and equipment. It was obvious both to John Dennis and his brother, who was winning many prizes in road and race-track bicycle competitions, that the 1896 Locomotives on Highways Act would rapidly revolutionize the motor-vehicle industry. Bicycles would be superseded by far more powerful machines – machines which they could see no valid reason for not manufacturing under the name of Dennis. For some months they were intrigued by the thought of a motor tricycle, and installed a De Dion engine into a tricycle frame. In August 1899 this motorized tricycle was tested up the steep slope of Guildford High Street where it was seen by a zealous constable who considered that it was proceeding at a reckless speed. In the magistrates' court the policeman insisted that the tricycle had been travelling at a minimum of 16 m.p.h. The magistrates came to the conclusion that the speed of 16 m.p.h. had not been proved and dismissed the charge, although a fine of twenty shillings was imposed for furious driving. The following morning a notice appeared in the window of the Dennis shop stating that on the sworn testimony of a police officer the tricycle had climbed Guildford High Street at 16 m.p.h.! Not content with manufacturing tricycles, the Dennis brothers built quadricycles which were fitted with De Dion Bouton motors, but the novelty of these machines was short-lived. By the end of the nineteenth century the Dennis brothers, along with Edwin Foden and many others, including thirty-two-year-old William Morris at Cowley, were convinced that the future of vehicles of the twentieth century was in high-powered motor cars and commercial vehicles.

William Morris was born in the parish of St John, Worcester, on 10th October 1877. His father, Frederick Morris, had emigrated to Canada at an early age, become an expert horseman and had driven the Royal Mail coach from Winnipeg to Toronto. Returning to England, he had married, worked for a time for a Worcester draper, and later taken up farming. In 1880 the Morris family moved from Worcester to Oxford owing to the fact that Frederick Morris's father-in-law was going blind and could no longer cope with the management of his farm at Headington. Young William Morris was sent to the local school where he remained until he was fifteen. He taught himself to ride a borrowed penny farthing, saved his pocket money and eventually bought a second-hand solid-tyred 'safety' bicycle of cross-framed design. This bicycle he continually dismantled and reassembled, thus acquiring the reputation of being mechanically minded. His ambition, however, was to study medicine and become a surgeon. These ambitions were dramatically altered in 1893 when his father's asthma compelled young William to leave school, become the family breadwinner, and take a job with a local firm of bicycle assemblers. Months later he set up on his own at a workshop in James Street, Cowley St John, repairing bicycles and selling accessories. One day the Rector of St Clement's asked him to build a bicycle for his use. As the Rector was a man of some considerable weight, the bicycle needed a 27-inch frame, and when built and successfully used became a visible advertisement for Morris's skill. By 1900 Morris had machined and built a single-cylinder $1\frac{3}{4}$ h.p. engine, using purchased castings which he had fitted into a frame for a motor cycle. The following year he moved his premises, announcing that he was 'W. R. Morris, Practical Cycle Maker and Repairer. 48 High Street and St James Oxford. Sole maker of the celebrated Morris Cycles.' Two years later he added 'Motor Repairs a Speciality'. During the next decade he suffered many setbacks and frustrations, but his resourcefulness and determination never deserted him. Many years later a story to illustrate his determination was told by Sir Miles Thomas as the Quadragenary Celebrations of the Institute of Automobile Engineers. Before the Stanley Show at the Agricultural Hall in Islington Morris worked for four days and four nights without sleep assembling his motor cycles. He managed to get the machines to the exhibition on time, and then caught an underground train on the Inner Circle line to return to his lodgings.

Hours later a porter shook the sleeping and exhausted form of Morris and demanded ' 'Ow many more times are you going round 'ere, Governor?'!

In 1912 he acquired new premises and land at Cowley – the premises including the school where his father had been educated – and became determined that he too would play a vital part in the future of Britain's motor industry.

2

On New Year's Eve 1900 a gale of almost hurricane strength blew across Britain. One of the massive stones on Stonehenge was dislodged by the force of the wind, and self-appointed prophets claimed that this mishap was an omen of ill-tidings for the future. Few took any notice of such misguided prophecies of gloom, but many were impressed by the forecasts of H. G. Wells, who at the age of thirty-three was renowned as a novelist, biologist and historian. In 1901 he claimed that 'the motor truck will be used for heavy traffic', and in his book which bore the long title of *Anticipations of the Reaction of Mechanical and Scientific Progress upon Human Life and Thought* he expounded his belief that a private car would be developed capable of a day's journey of 300 miles or more, and prophesied the building of arterial roads with 'traffic in opposite directions free to travel up to the limits of their very highest possible speed'. At the time that Wells was writing these words, Orville and Wilbur Wright were planning their first flight at Kitty Hawk, and man was about to begin his conquest of space. It was an exciting era, but Britain's leaders, complacently believing in her industrial supremacy, needed rousing from their lethargy to accept its challenge.

No less a man than Edison had rebuked Britain when he remarked: 'The motor car ought to have been British. You first invented it in the 1830s. You have roads only second to those in France. You have hundreds of thousands of skilled mechanics in your midst, but you have lost your trade by the same kind of stupid legislation and prejudice that has put you back in many departments of the electrical field.'

It required a speech at the Guildhall by the Duke of York, after his world tour, to awaken the nation to the demands of the new century. He advised people to emigrate, mentioned 'the hopeless struggle for existence which too often is the lot of many in the Old Country' and alluded to the fact that in the colonies these were doubts as to whether Britain could maintain her overseas trade against foreign competition. Fortunately England did wake up, possibly inspired by the words of 'Land of Hope and Glory' set to the pompous and patriotic music of Edward Elgar. The music stirred the hearts of all Englishmen, as did the news that Captain Scott was leading an expedition to the Antarctic, that the Boer War was ended, and that coronation preparations were gathering momentum. Enrico Caruso made his Covent Garden début and cricketing heroes such as Fry, Jessop and Ranjitsinhji thrilled the vast crowds at Lord's and the Oval in their matches against the strong Australian side. There were more than 4000 horse-drawn buses in London, and although less than thirty motor buses were beginning to usurp them, the most optimistic, willing to take a leaf out of H. G. Wells's book, forecast that the days of the horse-drawn vehicle were numbered. A quarter of a century had elapsed since the historian James Froude had written: 'No prudent man will venture a walk in London streets unless his will is made, his affairs in order, and a card case in his pocket that his body may be identified.' The London scene was changing. The majority of the roads were macadamized, and many of them were being relaid with wood blocks overlaid with a thin layer of asphalt which greatly reduced the noise level caused by the iron tyres of the vehicles which used them. By 1901 motor cycles – in reality modified pedal bicycles with engines clipped to the frame and driving the rear wheel by round belts – were adding to the congestion of private carriages, hansom cabs, growlers, tradesmen's carts and heavy drays. The Automobile Club of Great Britain and Ireland had been founded in 1897 and the Motor Union six years later. These organizations, joined by cycling associations, determined that the future of the motor industry and the transport of the country depended upon improved roads. Consequently the Roads Improvement Association was formed. Members included Hon. Arthur Stanley, M.P., Hon. John Scott-Montagu, M.P., and Earl Russell. As a result of their lobbying, Mr Balfour set up a Departmental Committee in 1902 presided over by the Parliamentary Secretary to the Local Government Board, John Grant Lawson, M.P. When the committee issued its report it proposed that for purposes of administration all roads throughout Britain should be divided into three classes.

    a. National roads.
    b. County roads.
    c. District roads.

The administration of the first category should become the responsibility of a special department of the Local Government Board. The second category should be under the jurisdiction of a body to be known as the County Highways Board, whilst the third remained in the care of District Councils.

Although the recommendations and proposals showed a farsighted appreciation of the problems they went unheeded due to the apathy of the Government and the Local Government Board. When Sidney and Beatrice Webb subsequently published their *Story of the King's Highway* it contained a revealing attack on the Local Government Board which was thoroughly deserved. Attacks were also made in the national daily Press against motor vehicles which were described as social juggernauts.* One contributor in the *Daily Telegraph* wrote a lurid account of motor vehicles desecrating the countryside:

. . . the motormania as now carried on is an audacious presumption upon the public indulgence. It is a usurpation, apart from the law, and to no little extent in spite of the law, of a privilege in practice such as never has been theoretically recognized by the political spirit of the country for centuries. It is time to put these unchartered libertines of locomotion in their proper place.

The scandal never was so obnoxious as it has become this season. The automobilists drive their machines as if they were the ironclads of the highway, bent upon ramming the enemy . . . every day these exponents of the new privilege become more reckless, more arrogant, more supercillious and rude, more indifferent to everyone's convenience but their own. If the danger to personal security has become a genuine one, the question of damage to public assets and private property cannot be disregarded. It is no longer possible to keep the roads watered. The dust is raised in continual clouds. It gets in your throat and your eyes. It envelopes you. You cannot avoid it. It reminds you of the famous and profound remark of the late Shah of Persia in the diary of his English visit: 'The ladies of Manchester do not wear white dresses; for if they wear them lo! they are suddenly black.' The particles upon the surface of the highway are pulverised by the incessant grinding of these juggernaut wheels . . . it is evident that the time has come when public opinion must

* According to *Webster's Dictionary*, the derivation of the word 'juggernaut' was from the Hindu idol whose temple, situated at Orissa, had a kind of movable pyramidal carriage 200 feet high. In former centuries pilgrims were accustomed to sacrifice themselves by falling between its wheels when it was in motion.

insist that the abuse of automobilism should be suppressed with the utmost determination. . . .

This letter created an avalanche of letters in similar vein. The correspondence lasted for more than a month, and included one letter from an eminent London specialist who stated that the brain damage caused by driving at speeds in excess of sixty miles an hour would inevitably lead to insanity and a lifetime spent in an asylum!

Despite such outcries, the first five years of the twentieth century proved to be a period of intensive development in the design of internal combustion engines for automobile use. By 1905 most of the unpractical designs for vehicles had been discarded, and the principle of a four- or six-cylinder engine under a bonnet in front, a change-speed gearbox, and a bevel or worm-driven live axle accepted. Allowing for such conformity, there were upward of 200 motor-car manufacturers in the country, the majority of whom assembled cars from components supplied by engine, gearbox and axle manu-facturers.

An article in the *Daily Mail* in April 1904 stated:

Britain is making a bold effort to beat France in the motor industry. English makers are increasing and are steadily evolving a car suitable for English roads, and combining the speed of the French cars with the stability of our own. Britain is well ahead in motor-van building and Thornycrofts have supplied several wagons to the German War Office. Trials are being made with motor-vans for the conveyance of mails, and next year the Automobile Club, in conjunction with the Society of Motor Manufacturers, will hold a series of light van trials.

During 1906 a Cambridge undergraduate, Harry Ricardo, began to make experiments in an attempt to cure the knocking of petrol engines. Borrowing a four-cylinder high-speed Daimler petrol engine he and Professor Bertram Hopkinson, years later described by Ricardo as 'the most brilliant, versatile and imaginative research leader I have ever come across', began a series of tests. To Ricardo's con-sternation the engine had to be returned before the tests were completed. For many years it was believed that the knock in the petrol engine was due to pre-ignition initiated by some hot surface within the combustion chamber, and this belief remained until Ricardo completed further experiments at Shoreham shortly before the outbreak of the First World War.

Notwithstanding the slow development of petrol engines, there is no doubt that the first years of the new century heralded the perma-nent establishment of the commercial vehicle industry, even though many companies were formed, temporarily flourished and at a later date fell into oblivion through bankruptcy, liquidation or amalgamation. One such firm was the Wolseley Company, whose history is so closely associated with the life of Herbert Austin, born at Little Missenden, Buckinghamshire, in 1866. His father, like William Morris's father, was a farmer whose livelihood was adversely affected by the economic depression of the 1870s. Loans from banks to tide farmers over the inevitable hard times were not easily obtained, and many smallholders were compelled to sell their land. Herbert's father, having suffered this misfortune, was given the job of farm bailiff at Earl Fitzwilliam's Wentworth Woodhouse estate in Yorkshire, where his brother was the estate architect. Herbert was sent to the local village school and later to the Grammar School at nearby Rotherham. He listened to his father playing the organ in the local parish church on Sundays, enjoyed drawing freehand and was encouraged by the praise given him by his teachers who recognized his talent as an artist. The one sadness which clouded his life was the death of his elder brother who fell down the stairs, fractured his leg and died from gangrene days later. After his brother's death Herbert went to Brampton Commercial College to complete his education before being apprenticed with the Great Northern Railway.

The intention that he should become a railway engineer was altered as a result of a visit to Wentworth Woodhouse of his uncle who had emigrated to Australia years previously. Spellbound by stories of the Bush Herbert did not hesitate when his uncle offered to take him with him on his return to Victoria where he was works manager to a general engineering firm in North Melbourne. Filled with enthusiasm Herbert may have had grandiose ideas that his uncle was responsible for a large factory, but the truth was that the entire works consisted only of a corrugated iron shed, a foundry and a small forge. Disillusioned soon after his arrival in Australia and disappointed with the work he was expected to perform, Herbert Austin soon left his uncle and spent the next two years working for Cowans, who were agents for printing machines and Crossley engines. In his spare time he completed designs and estimates which he submitted as an entry in a competition organized by the Victorian Government for a swing bridge over the Yarra river. He did not win the competition, but his entry received favourable mention.

On Boxing Day 1887 he married Helen Dron, daughter of Scottish emigrants. Days later he commenced a new working life as manager for an engineering company who were developing a sheep-shearing machine for Frederick York Wolseley, an inventor and brother of the famous Field Marshal. In 1891 the directors of the company offered Herbert the managership of the British company which had recently been formed in London to take over various of the Wolseley patents

This 4-ton standard Foden steamer, which was fitted with wood block brakes, left the factory in Sandbach on 24th November 1908 to enter service with Joseph Rank Ltd

This van, supplied to Carter Paterson in 1908, continued in service until 1932. Renovated by Leyland apprentices, it is in running order today

This picture appeared in *The Commercial Motor* in September, 1908 and shows the General Motorcab Company's Dennis lorry for breakdown and emergency service. The caption read: 'A winding drum is fitted and this is gear driven, from the shaft between the clutch and gearbox, through a worm and worm wheel. A vehicle weighing as much as two tons can be wound onto the lorry platform with ease.' *National Motor Museum, Beaulieu*

'The Pig', Leyland's first petrol-engined vehicle. *British Leyland*

This 5-ton Foden steam wagon of 1910 ran on steel wheels

Leyland lorry 1910–12, fitted with a live back axle, the casing of which contained double reduction gearing. *National Motor Museum, Beaulieu*

Leyland subsidy-type, 1914. Following the War Department trials of 1913, manufacturers were quick to advertise their government contracts. Leylands were no exception and in November of that year announced, "War Office testimony to Leyland efficiency. Vehicles already supplied – 65; New Order – 55; Total – 120.' *National Motor Museum, Beaulieu*

right Dennis, 1913/14. Dennis, along with Pagefield, were late entries into the War Department subsidy trials of 1913. These 30 h.p. Dennis were fitted with waterproof magnetos. *National Motor Museum, Beaulieu*

Napier 1-ton, *circa* 1914. *National Motor Museum, Beaulieu*

Daimler lorry assembly, *circa* 1914. *National Motor Museum, Beaulieu*

– the object being to improve the accuracy of construction of the sheep-shearing equipment which Australian manufacturers were unable to make to a sufficiently high standard.

Excited at the anticipation of the new job, Herbert and his wife sailed for England. As so often occurs in life anticipation proved better than realization, for he found that the state of affairs at the Wolseley factory in England was chaotic. He had been under the impression that the Wolseley Company manufactured the shearing machinery, but in reality many of the components were made by other firms and merely assembled by Wolseley. To make matters worse, several of the Midland engineering firms who were suppliers did not have the technical expertise to provide sufficiently tough component parts. Herbert's problems did not end once he appreciated this situation, for in addition the Wolseley factory was badly organized and held virtually no stock. Once he recovered from his initial disappointment, he quickly and forcibly began to remedy the situation. He took a far stronger line with suppliers, gave them exact details of his requirements and insisted that they abided by delivery dates. His colleagues found him obstinate in the face of difficulties and at times impulsive – as his purchase of larger premises in Aston without the permission of his directors illustrated – but they had no doubt as to his ability and initiative. He worked long hours without respite, and in his moments of leisure at the weekend took part in rallies and runs organized by the local bicycling club. On one Sunday his wife, objecting to being left alone so often, spiked both tyres of his bicycle with her hat-pin. He spent the entire day mending punctures!

In 1894 Herbert Austin visited Paris for the first time and almost certainly examined and admired some of the motor cars which had competed in the Paris–Rouen Trials. For the next two years he experimented with the designing and building of the first Wolseley Three Wheeler, which was exhibited at the Crystal Palace Exhibition in December 1896. The motor industry was still in its infancy, and inevitably Austin's growing reputation came to the ears of Frederick Simms. Simms, already acknowledged as a pioneer, had founded the Society of Motor Manufacturers and Traders. In 1895 his advice had been sought by the Royal Engineers Workshop at Chatham for engines to use on narrow-gauge railways and also for 2-ton motor lorries. During the next five years the War Office, in consultation with Simms and Vickers, decided that they should gain a foothold in the motor-car industry. As a result of these consultations, the Wolseley Tool and Motor Car Company was formed, and Herbert Austin was appointed general manager for a period of five years at a salary of £500 and a 5 per cent commission on the firm's profits. He remained with the company for four years, when he left to set up his own company, having found 'suitable premises' at Longbridge, seven miles south of Birmingham. The 'suitable premises' consisted of a small factory on $1\frac{1}{2}$ acres of land which had been derelict for four years. Cobwebs, grime and an air of desolation pervaded the premises, but Austin, with his appreciation of the problems of car production, was certain that it was ideal, not only because high-class paintwork finish could be carried out free from the smoke-laden atmosphere of Birmingham, but also because there was adjacent land suitable for factory expansion at a future date. By the time of the 1906 Motor Show at Olympia Austin had 270 employees at Longbridge and was producing ten cars a week. One weekend he envisaged, designed and modelled the Austin insignia – the wings representing speed and the little whorls depicting the clouds of dust which had been disturbed by the speed of the wheels.

Many years later Lord Brabazon of Tara wrote in his autobiography:

I cannot for the life of me recall exactly when or how I first met Herbert Austin, I think it was probably in 1903, he was rather older than I was and a big gun in the world. I was nineteen and dancing attendance on Charlie Rolls, but although it now seems great insolence, I never addressed him by any other name but Pa and I was Brab to him all his life. I don't know why I was instantly attracted to him, his dark clothes and bowler hat, his brusqueness and inability to suffer fools gladly, his directness and the patent fact that stood out – that he was a mechanic – nothing more nor less.

In the same year that Herbert Austin returned to England from Australia James Sumner inherited a small engineering works at Leyland in Lancashire. One of his ancestors, Elias Sumner, had been the village blacksmith at Leyland during the Napoleonic Wars, and the business had been handed down from father to son for almost a hundred years. By the time that James Sumner received his inheritance, the works produced iron castings up to half a ton and brass castings up to half a hundredweight, but was not a profitable concern. Sumner found that his inheritance included debts and an antiquated horse-shoeing appliance which he believed was outdated and surplus to his requirements. Wise before his time, he was convinced that the future would show that machines and not horses would provide the motivating force of transport. In his desire to experiment he bought a second-hand tricycle, called a Starley Sociable since it had two seats side by side, from Squire Bretherton of Runshaw Hall. He fitted the tricycle with a small twin-cylinder engine and oil-fired boiler, which so impressed the Squire when he visited Sumner that he gave the astounded mechanic a shilling! Tested on the road the tricycle infuriated the police, but the local magistrates, understanding that the machine went far too fast for a man with a red flag to remain ahead of it, merely imposed a nominal fine of one shilling plus costs when a prosecution was brought. Undeterred by this setback, Sumner dismantled the engine and installed it in a lawn mower presented to him by Robert Frisby, head gardener at Worden Hall. The mechanized lawn mower proved successful, winning first prize and silver medal at the Royal Lancashire Agricultural Show. Sumner decided to concentrate on lawn mowers, and sales increased with orders placed by cricket clubs and by Rugby School. Many gardeners of large estates where the Leyland mowers were used still treated them in a similar manner to the horses which had previously pulled the mowers, and the cry 'Whoa' was heard more often than 'Stop'. It was evident, however, that the Leyland business was on the verge of prosperity, but equally evident that James Sumner needed additional capital to finance the expansion of his business interests. A company, J. Sumner Ltd, was formed with T. Coulthard & Co., a Preston engineering firm, taking over a half-share. Shortly after the new company was formed, George Spurrier, who was associated with Coulthards, joined Sumner and the decision was taken to produce steam wagons in addition to lawn mowers. On August Bank Holiday 1896, less than a fortnight before the Locomotives on Highways Bill received the Royal Assent, his younger brother Henry Spurrier returned from Florida, where he had been working as a railway draughtsman when not hunting big game in the frozen north of Canada. Born at Marston-in-Dove in Derbyshire, he had been educated at Uppingham before being apprenticed to Fletchers, a firm of Manchester engineers. Feeling a sense of wanderlust, he forsook England for America, where for some years he roamed the continent to his heart's content – and for good measure married an American! On his return he became intrigued by his brother's interest in the Sumner Company and offered his help. A man of dynamic personality, with a sound knowledge of practical engineering to support it, his help proved invaluable. Before Christmas he had persuaded his father, a retired business man who had become a landowner and farmer, to put up capital and form the Lancashire Steam Motor Co. with four partners, Henry Spurrier, Snr, Henry Spurrier, Jnr, George Spurrier and James Sumner.

The new company moved to a small factory in Herbert Street, Leyland, where twenty men were employed. The day's work began at 6.15 a.m. when the employees were summoned by the ringing of a handbell. In those far distant days it was possible to buy a pint of beer from the local public house on the way to work, and many of the workers would drink a draught of ale before commencing their day's labour. Breakfast would often be bread, butter and sardines, with tea

43

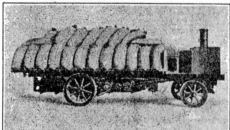

from cans warmed on the furnace by permission of the ever-popular brass founder. There was an hour's break for lunch and work finished at 5.45 p.m., except on Saturday when the final bell was sounded at 11.45 a.m. For a total week's work of sixty-three hours the employees would earn twenty-eight shillings. In 1898 vehicles built at the Herbert Street works won two £100 prizes in the open competitions of the Liverpool Self-Propelled Traffic Association and the Royal Agricultural Society of England. The RAS competition was held at Sutton Coldfield near Birmingham, and William Sumner wrote:

I was appointed to drive this wagon and I had for a mate Ted Hamer, a young apprentice. It was a last-minute rush, as these things usually are, to get everything ready and so we had to travel late on our first day out from the works towards our destination.

About ten o'clock at night I thought it time to look out for lodgings, so I pulled up at a wayside inn but was dismayed to find it closed as we were now in Cheshire and closing time was earlier than in Lancashire.

So I banged on the door until a man appeared at the window above and asked us what the devil we wanted. I said we wanted lodgings for the night, whereupon he told us to go to hell and he shut the window.

We discovered a barn with plenty of hay; but it was already occupied with a party of Irish labourers. I put out the lamp and we dossed down as far away from them as possible. I don't think we slept much as I had a fair amount of money and was afraid of being robbed.

However, we arose early and somewhat refreshed, ordered breakfast at the inn and after a wash and feed we were on the road again in good time. We had to reach our destination that day and be on the showground before 6 p.m. or be disqualified, and we did it with only a few minutes to spare.

It was typical of Henry Spurrier, Jnr, that he insisted that some of the prize money be spent on an outing for the entire works staff, taking them and their wives on a trip to Lake Windermere, followed by a dinner in a nearby hotel. With instinctive foresight he realized the dividends payable by maintaining the happiest relationship with those who toiled on his behalf. One incident typified his attitude towards the employees. A man was sacked by the foreman for smoking at work, and sadly went to Henry Spurrier to collect his cards. Spurrier asked him if he really was able to smoke and work at the same time. When the answer was in the affirmative Spurrier handed the man a cigar, told him to get back to work, but warned him that if his work suffered he would have to leave the firm.

In many respects Henry Spurrier, Jnr, was a man far in advance of his time. As a result of the success of his company in these and other Trials, he found that orders were constantly being received for vehicles, and on one occasion was heard to remark with a brashness reminiscent of his life in America: 'We've got the world by the pants and a downhill pull.'

By 1902 a new works was built on a three-acre site, and twelve months later the firm was registered privately under the Limited Liability Act with an authorized capital of £50000. The new and larger premises were rendered necessary to keep pace with the growing output, and another site at Leyland was purchased covering over seven acres. The old works were still used for boiler-making, woodworking, and for the tinsmith's and foundry work, while the new works, all on the ground floor, with the exception of the offices, were divided into three bays, each 200 ft long with saw-tooth glazed roofs. One bay was reserved for machine tools, one bay for the fitters' and tool room, and one provided with a travelling crane for erecting. Behind the offices were the stores and an extension at the rear was utilized for painting. The two works found employment for 160 hands, and were capable of an output of about five wagons per month. Power for driving was supplied by a 30 h.p. gas engine, and the machine tools, chiefly of British make, were driven by overhead shafting.

The passing of the Motor Car Act of 1903 further advanced Leyland's progress. In 1905 the company manufactured twenty-five steam wagons and sixteen petrol wagons, in addition to receiving their first order for a London double-decker bus. In those days the petrol wagons would go out heavily loaded with 2-gallon cans to meet their needs *en route*, whilst on long journeys the drivers of the steam wagons would, of necessity, keep an eye open for brooks and streams where water could be replenished, and depots where coal could be bought. In 1907 the name of the company was altered to the one word Leyland.

3

By 1905 Edwardian England was a nation of contrasts. Industry was booming, with the shipyards bursting at the seams with orders and the Lancashire cotton trade enjoying an unprecedented world demand for their goods. The aristocracy and the affluent led a life of extravagant luxury, yet ironically hunger and starvation were known to hundreds of thousands. Twenty thousand unemployed and their wives held a rally in Hyde Park and marched through the streets of London under banners headed 'Bread for our Children'. George Bernard Shaw denounced unemployment and starvation in his new play *Major Barbara,* clamouring that poverty was the worst crime and that by comparison all other crimes were tantamount to virtues. Matches were threepence for a dozen boxes and cigarettes five for a penny. The pound was a shining golden sovereign and not a mere piece of paper.

If any proof was needed that the commercial vehicle industry was becoming a sturdy child, the publication of a new magazine *The Commercial Motor* provided it. The founder of the magazine was Edmund Dangerfield, owner of the Temple Press Ltd, and a pioneer in the field of technical publications, the first of which he had produced in 1891. In his youth an enthusiastic cyclist, he had published papers giving news of both cycling and motor cycling. Encouraged by the success of these magazines, he envisaged the need for a paper to deal exclusively with commercial vehicles. The first issue was published on 16th March 1905 under the editorship of Edward

Shrapnell Smith, who was a founder member of the Automobile Club, a director of the Car and General Insurance Co., and hon. secretary of the Liverpool Self-Propelled Traffic Association which he had formed with Lord Derby, Sir David Salomons and Frederick Simms. Shrapnell Smith, born in 1875 and educated at Liverpool Royal Institution School, had been apprenticed in the chemical industry and had spent several years working as a research chemist. Fascinated by the development of road transport, he had been one of the 350 people who had attended a meeting at the Cannon Street Hotel on 10th December 1895 when the Self-Propelled Traffic Association was formed, and had been appointed conductor of the Lancashire Heavy Motor Vehicle Trials held in 1898, 1899 and 1901. In 1903 he helped to establish the Motor Van and Wagon Users Association of which he became hon. treasurer. Subsequently the name of the association was changed to the Commerical Motor Users Association. It was an inspired choice of Dangerfield's to appoint Shrapnell Smith to be editor of the new magazine. Dedicated to his task, and with an unrivalled knowledge of the youthful commercial vehicle industry, he was to play a vital part in it for the next forty-seven years. Always smartly dressed, and with a great sense of humour, he was a character who possessed certain eccentricities. To his editorial staff and to his linotype operators and compositors he was known as 'the comma king'. He would never dictate from his chair, but would pace up and down whilst dictating to his secretary. It was his invariable habit to dictate the punctuation – the words 'comma', 'colon', 'semi-colon' and 'full stop' being interspersed whenever necessary.

At the time that the first issue of *The Commercial Motor* appeared there were only 3000 commercial vehicles in use, the majority of which were steamers. There were less than fifty petrol-driven vehicles capable of carrying a load of two tons, and of these less than a dozen which could carry a load in excess of four tons. Pneumatic tyres were unknown for commercial vehicles, which were shod either with steel tyres or solid rubber tyres. The first issue, of which 20000 copies were printed, price one penny, described itself on the title page as 'The Authority on The Van, The Lorry, The Agricultural Motor, The Omnibus and The Public Service Vehicle'. There were articles on 'Light Delivery Vans', 'The Experience of Messrs Pickford Ltd', 'The Views of the Hon. Arthur Stanley, M.P.', and 'The Forthcoming Show at the Agricultural Hall, which anticipated the largest display of commercial vehicles ever known. Amongst the advertisers were the Lancashire Steam Motor Co., who stated that they were makers of steam and petrol vehicles for freight, passenger and municipal uses, to comply with the Local Government Board

New Regulations, and proudly announced that they had won two £100 prizes, nine gold and silver medals and provided special vehicles to suit colonial requirements. The Wolseley Tool and Motor Car Co., in their front-page advertisement, mentioned that they supplied chemical fire-engines, motor ambulances, petrol locomotives, public service omnibuses, tipping wagons and light tram cars.

The show at the Agricultural Hall was an outstanding success. Foden's exhibited two of their latest standard 5-ton steam wagons and sold them to Mark Mayhew Ltd, a firm of Battersea flour millers. Thornycrofts sold lorries to the Worksop and Retford Brewery and Mann Crossman and Paulin bought Lancashire Steam Motor Co. lorries to transport their beer from the brewery to their public houses. Each wagon could carry twenty-five barrels alone, or twenty barrels on its platform and another ten barrels on a trailer. The usual daily trip of each lorry was seven miles outwards and return twice a day. Three years earlier Fodens had made a wagon for the Henley brewers W. H. Brakspear which had been named 'The Busy Bee'. During the year the brewers announced:

Our wagon was built for us by Messrs Foden and Son of Sandbach in the summer of 1902. The upkeep was estimated at £1 per week, and during the first few months it was about this, as being one of the first patterns, many improvements had been added. Last year our total repair bill was £1 15s. We tested our wagon and trailer up to eight tons load, although in actual work we limit our load to six tons. We burn (full and empty) one hundredweight of coal per eight miles. We estimate the wagon to replace five horses, but as she takes all the long journeys and so relieves the other horses she really saves much more. During the whole time we have used the wagon we have always found her above the work, and no hill seems too steep for her.

It was noticeable too that commercial firms were beginning to realize the value of using the panels of their vehicles to advertise their goods and products. Milnes-Daimler built a van for Nestles Food with slogans on the sides, and another for John Broadwood and Sons, pianoforte makers, with a huge painting of a grand piano along the length of the vehicle. Harrods had purchased three Peugeot vans and three Milnes-Daimler vans which were doing much to alleviate the time spent in delivering parcels and orders. Before one run the porter was bemoaning his fate, and murmuring that as the delivery was not to start until 3 p.m. and the run was to take him as far as Wimbledon Common, then he would not be back before 9 p.m. as there were seventeen places to visit. To his delight and astonishment, he was back at Harrods by 6.15 p.m.! Royal Mail vans, four-cylinder vehicles carrying eight hundredweight, were in use and averaged sixty miles a day in London postal services. For the most part, such vans were not considered difficult to drive, although the heavier steam vehicles were thought to need both skill and strength. One firm of road locomotive engineers held a heavy-lorry drivers' competition for which more than 200 applications were received. Elimination trials resulted in the winning driver being a boy of sixteen, much to the sponsor's consternation. Despite such a shock result, it was realized that the basic capabilities required in a first-class driver were a care in the fuel consumption of his vehicle and the speed with which he could manipulate his locomotive. Stokers retired from the Royal Navy and Merchant Navy were considered ideal as prospective drivers, for they were 'used to discipline, and accustomed to keeping themselves clean'. It was suggested that a competent and experienced driver was worth a weekly wage of thirty shillings.

Many firms found it easier to employ new drivers for their motorized delivery vans rather than to persuade their old hands, accustomed to horse-drawn vehicles, to take an interest in modern machines. Messrs Peek Frean, the biscuit-makers, were a typical example. When they introduced two-cylinder 10 h.p. vans, their drivers were reluctant to learn how to handle the 'new-fangled things' and their prejudices were so deep-rooted that drivers with engineering experience were employed. Soon after Peek Frean

'OPELESS!

"'Omeless, 'ungry, and not an 'orse's 'ead to 'old!"

bought these vans, an incident occurred to illustrate the superiority of mechanical traction. As some road work was in progress a Peek Frean van was compelled to make a detour taking in a short steep rise known as Morden Hill which had a very loose road surface. Halfway up the hill a pair-horse team attached to a cartload of flour in sacks was floundering, with the horses' hooves unable to grip the uneven surface. Whilst the perspiring cart driver struggled to get his horses to pull the cart around, the Peek Frean van sailed up the hill past the exhausted horses and carter to the cheers of the bystanders.

As more and more firms decided to purchase commercial vehicles, the advice of the pioneers was eagerly sought by company directors. A. W. Gamage, owner of the Holborn store, approached his great friend Edmund Dangerfield, and on his advice purchased six delivery vans from James and Browne Ltd of Hammersmith. Another van built by this firm was for Mr Heinz of '57 Varieties' fame. Mr Heinz was so enthralled by seeing his van being built that he went to the factory every day to watch the progress in its manufacture. One of the sleeping partners of James and Browne Ltd was Mr R. S. Roget, a grandson of the compiler of the famous *Thesaurus*.

Leyland in their 1905 catalogue listed many of the Heavy Motor Car Orders issued the previous year:

HEAVY MOTOR CAR ORDER, 1904
(ABRIDGED.)

Light Locomo-tive or Heavy Motor Car	The expression 'Light Locomotive or Heavy Motor Car' means a mechanically-propelled road vehicle, weighing, unladen, over 2 tons and under 5 tons.
Trailer	The expression 'Trailer' means a vehicle drawn by a light locomotive or a heavy motor car.
Registration	Every heavy motor car must be registered with the Council of a County or the Council of a County Borough.
	The owner must be prepared to give particulars as to:
	(A) The unladen weight = U.W. tons.
	(B) The axle weight of each axle = A.W. tons.
	(C) The diameter and width of each wheel.
Fees	The registration fee for a heavy motor car, used for trade purposes only, is £1, and does not require renewing annually.
Identification Marks	The registered number must be placed in a conspicuous position in front and at the back of the car and on the back of the trailer when such is being drawn by a car or tractor.
	A trailer does not require registering.
Licenses	No license is required for a heavy motor car which is used exclusively for carrying goods.

Driver	A driver must take out a license, which costs 5s., and it must be renewed annually. If he resides in a County Borough he must apply to the chief constable; otherwise to the County Council Offices.
Weight Unladen	Weight unladen does not include water in the boiler or tanks, oil in the oil bath, fuel, or any detachable sides or other accessories not essential to the working of the machine.
Total Weight of Car and Trailer	The combined unladen weight of the motor vehicle must not exceed 5 tons and of a motor and trailer 6½ tons.
Axle Weight	Axle weight means the aggregate weight transmitted to the road by the several wheels attached to any one axle of the motor car or trailer when such car or trailer is loaded.
	The axle weight of car and load must not exceed 12 tons, and the weight transmitted to the road by any axle must not exceed 8 tons.
Tyres	The tyre of each wheel of a heavy motor car shall be smooth, and where the tyre touches the road it must be flat, excepting that the edges of the tyres may be rounded or bevelled on each edge to the extent of half an inch.
	The tyres may, however, be constructed of separate plates, the space between each plate must be parallel, and such space must not measure more than one-eighth of the width of the tyre, when the measurement is taken across the face of the tyre, in a line with the axle.
Width of Tyres and Diameter of Wheels	The width of a tyre of a heavy motor car must not be less than 5-in. and, in the case of a trailer, not less than 3-in. (if the trailer weighs, unladen, more than a ton).
	NOTE.—If a purchaser proposes to use a trailer not specially designed for motor work, he should consult us as to the width of tyres, etc.
	The width of tyres varies according to the diameter of wheel and axle weight.
Speed	The speed of a heavy motor car must not exceed 5 miles per hour if it weighs, unladen, over 3 tons, or the registered weight of any axle exceeds 6 tons, or if used to draw a trailer.
	With pneumatic tyres or tyres of soft material, and if the axle weight does not exceed 6 tons, 12 miles per hour is allowed; if over 6 tons axle weight, the speed may be 8 miles per hour if the tyres are of soft or elastic material.
Trailers	Trailers must have painted on the right or off side in letters and figures not less than one inch in height, the weight of trailer unladen=U.W. tons, and the axle weight of each axle=A.W. tons, if the trailer weighs unladen more than one ton.

	A trailer must be hung upon suitable springs. The axle weight of any trailer must not exceed 4 tons.
Brakes	A heavy motor car shall have two independent brakes; the reversing gear is now officially recognised as a second brake.
Width of Motor or Trailer	No heavy motor car or trailer shall exceed 7-ft. 6-in. width over all.

Orders for vehicles kept the manufacturers busy, but nevertheless the question of whether to use motor vans or horses was a constant problem over which there was endless argument. At a meeting of the Westminster City Council in July 1907 the Highways Sub-Committee brought up financial details for the committee to discuss on the merits of purchasing motor vans or horses. The details were:

TWO MOTORS	£	s.	d.
Wages of four motor drivers at 35 shillings per week	364	0	0
Coke—say 13 cwt per week per motor	60	0	0
Oils and sundries	28	0	0
Repairs, £65 each	130	0	0
Annual Cost	£582	0	0
Capital cost of two motors	£1200	0	0

HORSES			
Fodder for five horses, at 12 shillings per week per horse	156	0	0
Shoeing, at £3 10 each per annum	17	10	0
Wages of five carmen, at 28 shillings per week	314	0	0
Hiring five horses and drivers at 8 shillings and 8 pence per day (243 days)	526	10	0
Annual Cost	£1014	0	0
Capital cost of five horses at £70	£350	0	0

In the course of the discussion on these figures one member of the committee complained that the Highways Committee had been authorized to spend a certain annual sum on horses, and that sum should be spent irrespective of the merits of motor vans! His complaint was overruled. Tenders for motor vans had been received from six manufacturers including Fodens, who quoted a price of £570, less a discount of 5 per cent for two vehicles, and the Lancashire Steam Co. who quoted £580 plus an annual maintenance charge of £65 per van, and whose quote was accepted by the City Council despite a further complaint that the Highways Sub-Committee was the only committee of the Council to have exceeded its estimated for the year.

Although the majority of heavy commercial vehicles were powered by steam, every year found more petrol-driven motors on the road. Advertisements in magazines advised motorists as to how they could buy their petrol. One advertisement read:

It's Perfect Purity – that's the Point
SHELL
Every Can Sealed

whilst another stated:

Motor Spirit for Commercial Purposes
Delivered in Steel Barrels
and Railway Tank Barrels
Meade-King, Robinson and Co.
Old Hall St. Liverpool.

Despite such advertisements there were doubts as to the future supplies of petrol. In an effort to reassure customers an article was written in *The Commercial Motor* on the subject. The article ended: '... as to the continuance of supplies of Eastern spirit, there can be no doubt that there will be a sufficient supply from this source, so far as human foresight can judge, to last for many years, and the facilities for the transport being great, its use should tend to increase'.

Where private individuals were concerned, more and more were realizing the advantages of owning a commercial vehicle for business purposes. Mr Graham, who was a music-hall artist presenting a marionette show, and who needed bulky stage paraphernalia for his act, bought a Jackson van with a 9 h.p. single-cylinder engine for £200. Using this van, he left his Brixton home at 6 p.m., drove ten miles to Hampstead for his first performance, thence to Camberwell, then to Mount Street West, before returning to the Camberwell Palace for the second house. After finishing at the Palace he went to the Lambeth Baths, before making his final appearance for the night at the London Pavilion in Piccadilly Circus. If he had relied on horse-driven cabs he would have only been able to make three instead of six appearances each night. In his opinion his commercial vehicle paid for itself in six months.

On a larger scale one of the partners in Shoolbred's, the well-known Tottenham Court Road emporium, explained in an interview:

We have only one hundred less horses than before we bought our first motor, but we are doing enormously more work ourselves, and with infinitely greater satisfaction to our customers, who appreciate both the

54

directness and promptness of our delivery. The 31 motor vans replace 124 horses, and two of our larger Lacre vans, in one day, delivered $3\frac{1}{2}$ tons of furniture from Tottenham House to a few miles beyond Abingdon in Oxfordshire. This was a 60-mile run out, fully loaded, with a three hour stop at the house, and a 60-mile run home, after which both vans were out as usual the next morning . . . Some of our vans do as much as 24,000 miles a year, although the average is 17,000. All repairs to chassis and body, including renewal of rubber tyres, cost $1\frac{1}{4}$ pence per mile. Motor spirit, purchased in bulk, costs $\frac{3}{4}$d. per mile, and depreciation, drivers' wages, standing room, washing, oil, grease and insurance (third party claims) cost 3 pence per mile. The exact cost of our pair horse vans, for a maximum yearly mileage of 14,000 miles, worked out at $6\frac{1}{2}$ pence per mile, so by using motor vans we get an additional 3000 miles a year from each van at less cost.

Repairs to vans needed considerably more skill than many mechanics and engineers possessed. Butchery by some car repairers became prevalent to such an extent that one advertiser, who believed that lathes sold by his company would obviate such rough handling, headed his newspaper advertisement 'Kill the car butcher'. This resulted in his receiving a letter which read: 'Dear Sir, I see that you are advertising for a car butcher and none of my friends can tell me what you mean. But if you are wanting a man to destroy cars I beg to apply for the post, for I am a powerful man and can kill anything. Do you intend to pay by the job or by the day? If by the day how many cars should I be expected to destroy in the day?'

One of the problems confronting designers and builders of commercial vehicles was lack of capital. The dealings of a handful of slick financial tycoons had sickened and disheartened many prospective investors who would have liked to believe in the future prosperity of the youthful motor industry. Consequently very little capital was forthcoming to support the pioneers. Nor was it easy to find engineers capable of undertaking the work of designing commercial motors. Marine engineers and locomotive engineers were offered the task, but failed to adapt their knowledge and skill to a totally new industry. Engineering firms frequently produced impossible machines – one being a car in which the engine was placed as high as possible in a vehicle with exceptionally large wheels and high body. The object of this design was to raise the centre of gravity to the highest point. The car proved a dangerous failure. Another problem in the first decade of the century was the difficulty in persuading the British iron foundries to produce such light and complicated castings as motor cylinders. Steel casters were no more efficient in the early days, and at least one reputable firm claimed that it was impossible to cast anything in steel if it was less than half an inch thick.

Spring-makers, however, invariably produced better-quality springs than any of their continental rivals. The National Physical Laboratory, in their efforts to help, carried out tests and experiments using aluminium for the manufacture of crankcases and other parts, with the light alloy proving very satisfactory. At the same time experiments were being carried out to improve road surfaces and the Road Improvement Association offered prizes in 1907 for suitable tar spreading machines and preparations of tar. One of the pioneer counties in the improvement of road surfaces was Kent, chiefly due to the enthusiasm of the County Surveyor, H. P. Maybury. Local Councils and Corporations not only realizing the importance of improving the surface of roads, but were also beginning to show interest in commercial vehicles for municipal work. In 1909 a road sweeper which proved an instant success with Corporations was built by the Lacre Company at their new works at Letchworth. The company had been established in 1902 with the original name of the Long Acre Motor Car Company, a name which was altered to the simplified Lacre shortly after incorporation but before agreement was reached with the Scottish commercial vehicle manufacturers Albion for Lacre to act as their English distributors.

During the year 1905 another of the famous commercial vehicle firms was founded – Atkinsons. It would not be an exaggeration to claim that the existence of Atkinsons was caused by cotton and the need for mill machinery to power the cotton mills of North-West England. By the year 1887 Edward Atkinson and his elder brothers Harry, Samuel and Steven had left school and were working in mills near Preston. At the age of fourteen Edward secured an apprenticeship in the engineering trade with Coulthards, due to the influence of his father who was an experienced textile engineer with worldwide knowledge of installing looms. When Edward's apprenticeship was completed seven years later he was a fully trained and skilful millwright. In 1905 he married, left Coulthards and joined a firm of mill engineers in Kay Street, Preston. Countless engineers throughout the length and breadth of the country were realizing the potential of motorized vehicles for use on the highways as a form of transport, and were experimenting with the manufacture of cars. Edward Atkinson's employers planned to compete, and produced the Preston Pullcar, designed by Horace Viney. Edward, excited by the prospects of car manufacture, decided to start up on his own despite the fact that he had little or no capital. However, this lack of capital necessitated his relying for his income upon the one trade that he knew – mill engineering. As he prospered so he took on additional labour, but the basic trade that he carried on was mill repairs, either on the site or in his own workshop in Kendal Street, Preston. Gradually his

Alldays and Onions, *circa* 1914. The Alldays and Onions Pneumatic Engineering Company Limited were mainly involved with the production of power hammers and drop stamps etc. Between 1898 and 1914, however, the company's factory, Hatchless Works, Birmingham, produced a series of light goods vehicles and agricultural tractors. *National Motor Museum, Beaulieu*

This Foden steam wagon with a 5-ton tipper body and self-loading crane was delivered to the County Borough of Salford in 1914

Karrier Car, 1914. *National Motor Museum, Beaulieu*

Several of these 5-ton Foden steamers, manufactured between 1914 and 1915, were operated by Sunflour Mills Co. Ltd

The end of the journey for this crashed Fowler. *National Motor Museum, Beaulieu*

The popular 7½-cwt. Model T Ford van, *circa* 1915. *National Motor Museum, Beaulieu*

Leyland G-type, 1920. *National Motor Museum, Beaulieu*

Leyland, *circa* 1921. *National Motor Museum, Beaulieu*

Crossley lorries pulling the coffins of victims of the R38 airship tragedy, 1921. *National Motor Museum, Beaulieu*

Leyland overtype tipper of the early 1920s. *National Motor Museum, Beaulieu*

Several Fodens operated by Higgs & Hill Ltd, London, 1922. *National Motor Museum, Beaulieu*

engineering skill, allied to the fact that he efficiently carried out repairs to motor cars and vans of all shapes and sizes led to his participating to a greater extent in the motor-car industry.

In the autumn of 1907 the first Commercial Motor Show was held at Olympia. It was considered by the organizers to have been a success for 167 firms exhibited, and 21 000 visitors attended it. The promoters were sufficiently satisfied to stage the second show twelve months later. Only one other show, that of 1913, was held in the years prior to the First World War.

By the year 1908 many economists, industialists and pioneer motorists were beginning to take stock of the commercial vehicle industry, which had been in existence for twelve years if the passing of the 1896 Locomotives on Highways Act was accepted as its birthdate. In November 1908 Edward Shrapnell Smith read a paper entitled 'Twelve Years' Progress in the Application of Commercial Vehicles' to the Royal Automobile Club, with Sir David Salomons in the chair. In the course of his lecture Shrapnell Smith mentioned that in July 1895 the proprietors of the magazine *The Engineer* had announced a 1100-guinea competition for motors of all classes. Two of the classes in the competition, in respect of which prizes of £400 were offered, were open to commercial vehicles. One of these was for a vehicle which should be capable of carrying not more than one ton of goods in addition to the driver, and of which the gross weight should not exceed two tons; the other was open to vehicles which were capable of carrying five hundredweight of goods, in addition to the driver, and which did not weigh more than one ton gross. When the competition was held, only one entry out of seventeen entries in the commercial section appeared at Crystal Palace. It was a bitter disappointment for the promoters, a disappointment shared by Shrapnel Smith.

When members who had heard Shrapnell Smith's paper discussed it in debate one claimed that the most significant feature had not been sufficiently highlighted. He pointed out that although the speaker had given details of the increase of commercial vehicles in use in 1908 compared with 1902, he had virtually overlooked the facts that commercial vehicles represented less than $\frac{1}{2}$ per cent of the total number of horse-drawn vehicles in the country, and that there was not reliable proof that they were more economic than horses. The recent troubles caused to him in a proposed amalgamation with a French carrying business could be taken as an example. In 1906 the French company had spent £25 000 on self-propelled vehicles, and had been compelled to scrap the entire fleet due to faulty workmanship, whilst the English company were discovering that horse-drawn vehicles still had advantages over motor vehicles. In his opinion, although the future might produce more efficient self-propelled vehicles, at the present time they were inadequate.

Manufacturers of commercial vehicles naturally took a jaundiced view of such criticism, as they pressed forward with their plans. At Fodens the chairman, Edwin Foden, believing that 'the man who has no music in his soul cannot possibly be an engineer' had established a works brass band which was rapidly acquiring a high local reputation. The reason for the creating of the band was derived from the fact that at the time of the Relief of Mafeking, when jubilant celebrations were held in every town and village in England, Edwin Foden was a Sandbach councillor. He asked his fellow councillors if the Sandbach band could play at the Foden works party. The reply was in the negative as the band had other engagements, so Edwin Foden returned to his Elworth works and announced at the party, 'I've been to Sandbach and asked the Council if the band can come down here and play for an hour. The Council have said, "No, we want it in Sandbach", so I will tell you what I am going to do. I'm going to have a band of our own at Elworth.' Mr Rimmer of Southport became the band master and £800 was spent on the purchase of musical instruments. With the exception of the conductor every member of the band was an employee of Fodens – either a joiner, fitter, moulder or pattern-maker. The only criticism of the band was the name, the Foden Steam Wagon Works Brass Band, which by any standards was a mouthful. One of those who played a euphonium in the band was young William Foden. His father said to him one day: 'Willie, I am going to have the best band in the country. You are not quite equal to this standard so you must get out.' After winning many local prizes the band entered for the great band contests at Belle Vue, Manchester, and at Crystal Palace in London. When the band returned in triumph after their first victory at Crystal Palace many of the Elworth workers went out five miles with decorated lorries and cars to greet their heroes returning in the band coach. The band were transferred to the decorated lorries and hundreds of excited workers on bicycles escorted them to Sandbach. The Mayor came to welcome them together with the directors of Fodens who provided a slap-up dinner to celebrate the success.

4

What ought to have been far reaching developments for roads were introduced by Mr Lloyd George who had become the Chancellor of the Exchequer in 1908. Before he introduced his first Budget he was given to understand by both the Automobile Club and the Motor Union that they would advise their members to accept the payment of motor taxes provided that the proceeds of such taxes were used for the development and improvements of roads.

On 29th April in his Budget speech the Chancellor proposed firstly that money should be raised and placed at the disposal of a new central authority for constructing new roads to be called the Road Board, and secondly that grants should be made to local authorities for the purpose of carrying out plans for the widening and straightening of roads:

I propose that a beginning should be made this year with a scheme for dealing with the new but increasingly troublesome problem of motor traffic in this country. We are far ahead of all other European countries in the number of motor vehicles upon our roads. I look forward to a great future for this industry and I am the last to wish to hinder its development or to be responsible for proposals which would in any way be hostile to its interests. Quite the reverse. I am anxious to be helpful to its growth and prosperity. But I cannot help feeling that this problem is urgent and calls for immediate action. Any man who considers the damage which is done to the roads of this country, often by men who do not contribute to the upkeep of the roads they help so effectively to tear up; the consequent rapid increase in the expense of road maintenance; the damage done, if not to agriculture, at least to the amenities of rural life; by the dust clouds which follow in the wake of these vehicles; above all the appalling list of casualties to innocent pedestrians, especially to children, must come to the conclusion that this is a question which demands immediate notice at the hands of the Central Government. The question of road construction which was at one time deemed to be part of the essential development of the country, seemed to have been almost finally disposed of by the railways, but the advent of the motor has once more brought it to the front. It is quite clear that our present system of roads and of road making is inadequate for the demands which are increasingly made upon it by the new form of traction. Roads are too narrow, corners are too frequent and and too sharp, high hedges have their dangers and the old metalling admirably suited as it was to the vehicles we were accustomed to, is utterly unfitted to the motor car. Both the motorists and the general public are crying out for something to be done, and we propose to make a start. How the funds will be raised for the purpose it will be my duty later on to explain. . . . I have decided to base the new tax scale on the power of the cars and not on the weight. I have taken the advice of the Royal Automobile Club, and I fear that there is a schism in the ranks of automobilism on this point. . . . I now come to a second proposal that I have to make in this connection. I have already explained to the Committee that one of the chief reasons for imposing additional taxation on motor cars is the fact that the increase in their numbers necessitates a reorganisation of our main road system, and it will be obvious that were I to confine taxation to a mere readjustment of the scale of licence duties the burden would be imposed with absolutely no relation to the extent that the car might use the roads. . . . I therefore propose to put a tax of 3d. per gallon on petrol and other spirits used for motor vehicles . . . in order to meet the case of commercial vehicles, and vehicles such as motor cabs and omnibuses, which will not perhaps profit to so great an extent by the improvement in our roads, I propose to give a rebate of half the duty on the quantity used in their propulsion. . . .

Amongst those who opposed Lloyd George's proposals were three powerful groups. Firstly, Tory landowners, headed by Lord Robert Cecil and Mr Henry Chaplin. Cecil stated that in his opinion the road fund would produce a vast waste of public money and would be a grave danger for political corruption. The other two groups were those who desired a railway monopoly and those Treasury officials who disliked annual taxation being earmarked for specific purposes in advance. Although the measures of the Chancellor became law, they became little else, for his rivals and antagonists blocked his future schemes for road improvements by a combination of deliberate dilatoriness allied to a stubborn refusal to accept anything connected with the word progress.

The Road Board was formed in May 1910 and consisted of five members, all of whom were appointed by the Treasury. The first members were Sir George Gibb, formerly general manager of the North Eastern Railway who became chairman; Lord Pirrie, a ship-uilder; Sir John Macdonald, a man of seventy-four and president of the Scottish Automobile Club who on his own admission thought of his work as little more than a useful hobby; Lord St Davids; and Sir Charles Rose, Liberal M.P. for the Newmarket division of Cambridgeshire and an enthusiastic supporter of horse-racing who had bred Cyllene who became the sire of King Edward VII's Derby winner Minoru. Although the integrity and ability of the members of the Road Board was undisputed their knowledge of road problems was negligible. Despite at a later date it being announced in the House of Commons that the appointments had been made upon a territorial basis, many people believed that in reality the appointments had been made to mollify Lord Robert Cecil and to safeguard the interests of the railways.

Sir George Gibb's father had been a pupil of the great road builder Thomas Telford. His grandfather had carried out many commissions for Telford, including the building of the Glasgow to Carlisle road and the East India Dock Road in the East End of London, and had been the first road constructor to lay Aberdeen granite setts in the streets of London. Sir George Gibb, born in 1850 in Aberdeen and apprenticed to his father who was engineer to the North of Scotland Railway, eventually became general manager of the line, and in the first decade of the twentieth century one of the leading administrators of the underground railways of London. He had arranged for the Road Board to function from the London offices of the North Eastern Railway in Westminster which added fuel to the criticism of those who were convinced that the railways' future would always be given priority over any road improvements. One of those who was not happy at the manner in which the new Board's affairs were conducted was W. Rees Jeffreys who had been appointed Secretary to the Board at a salary of £1000 per annum. During 1911 a debate was held in the House of Commons about the powers, administration and future of the Board. As the debate unfurled, it became evident that very few members of the House had the remotest idea of either the functions of the Board or their achievements. The Press did little to publicize the Board's work and consequently the general public also had only a hazy notion of its record. In fact during the first twelve months of its existence the Board achieved little other than that part of the Fosse Way between Newark and Lincoln was resurfaced, and that a new experimental surface was laid down on the London–Folkestone road near Sidcup. Before the outbreak of the First World War the

Board had made a grant towards the new Croydon bypass and the Great West Road improvements, but that was virtually all. Possibly the root cause of the failure of the Board to achieve greater success was the stumbling block of the Treasury who mistrusted its powers.

On 6th May 1910 the Edwardian era ended with the death of the King. It was generally conceded that the new King was almost unknown to his subjects, although the *Daily Chronicle* carried an editorial which stated: 'The absolute blamelessness of his private life, his modesty and good nature, his insistent sense of duty, his frankness and honesty – these are fundamental attributes which show themselves in his face, his demeanour, his every speech and action of his career . . . the new Sovereign does his own thinking, is a man of decided views and will not hesitate to give expression to them when he is convinced that expression is necessary.' Before the end of the year the Hon. C. S. Rolls achieved fame as the first Englishman to fly the English Channel and a month later was tragically killed in an accident at the Bournemouth air display, Dr Crippen was arrested aboard the S.S. *Montrose*, Florence Nightingale died at the age o ninety, and the Bishop of Manchester was presented with a motor car. At the presentation he said: '. . . journeys will become a pleasure, and even a source of health, and if sometimes, through the inevitable breakdowns, your Bishop's arrival is delayed. . . .'

The coronation of King George V was held in Westminster Abbey on 23rd June 1911. A fortnight earlier a coronation parade was organized by the Commercial Motor Users Association, the Royal Automobile Club and the Society of Motor Manufacturers in London – a parade which brought together the greatest number of commercial vehicles ever assembled at any one time in the short history of the industry. One of the vehicles in the parade was the King's luggage van, which aroused considerable interest. Owing to the unprecedented demand upon printing houses, metal-workers and flag-makers due to the coronation events, the completion of the order for commemorative badges for those vehicles taking part was delayed, and on the day of the parade very few badges were available. When the parade was over the drivers of the vehicles and their wives were given a steak-and-kidney pie dinner at the Earls Court restaurant, with a total of 1200 being entertained.

Several of the vans in the parade were loaned by London stores, including Maples, who had bought a new fleet of motor vans in 1908. After tests and trials the directors decided to purchase two three-ton Leylands, four 2-ton Leylands and five 2-ton Dennis vans. The company's own van-building department was given the task o designing the bodies to be incorporated upon the chassis. New van depots were also acquired at Maidenhead, Wrotham, Berkhamsted

and Guildford. In total the Maples fleet consisted of thirty-three motor vans, 250 horses, 350 horse vans and two motor cars for their sales representatives. These two salesmen were well versed in the rules of the road, but like many other drivers were perturbed by the comments of a judge who remarked during the hearing of a case concerning a collision: 'There is no right or wrong side of the road for vehicular traffic. It is only by custom that certain of the rules of the road are recognized. They are, in fact, mere convention.' It was astounding that there were comparatively few serious accidents for the number of motor vehicles using the roads was rapidly increasing. More than 2100 motor vehicles were counted on the Chorley–Manchester road in one week, as compared to less than half that number during the same week in 1910. Vans were being used for every conceivable purpose of transport. One poulterer claimed: 'My 16 h.p. Albion van is used in the shooting season for game. There have been as many as 600 pheasants, and a couple of hundred hares and rabbits stacked in the capacious body, besides other trifles which have fallen to the guns. On other occasions the van has been used to take upward of forty children on a picnic outing.'

Although the coronation celebrations fired the patriotic fervour of the nation, behind the scenes there was considerable industrial unrest, much of it caused by a period of rising costs and prices at a time when wages remained low. In July 1910 there was a four-day railway strike in Newcastle, and less than two months later a lock-out of boiler-makers began on the North-East coast which lasted fourteen weeks and affected the ironworkers employed by the Federation of Ship-building Employers. A year later there was a seamen and firemen's strike which was settled by the employers who conceded higher wages and overtime rates. The success of the strikers made other unions take the attitude that they too might successfully strike for better conditions of work for their members. By mid-August the majority of the dockers in London, Liverpool and Manchester were on strike, and some railway porters came out in sympathy with the dockers. At Liverpool tempers flared, rioting ensued, the troops were called in, opened fire and killed two men. The Prime Minister, Herbert Asquith, perturbed by news from Germany, was anxious for peace at home, and was determined to avert a general strike. He acted quickly, but not before the North of England was paralysed by a rail strike which lasted four days and necessitated the troops again being called out.

The summer of 1911 was the hottest since 1868, and there was a lull in industrial unrest as miners, dockers and railway workers took their families to the seaside, basked in the sunshine, and enjoyed the delights of Blackpool and Scarborough. In the autumn the miners took a ballot on calling a general strike for minimum wage rates. When the result of the ballot was announced in January 1912 it gave the necessary majority for strike action and notices were sent out announcing a national stoppage at the end of February. On 1st March more than three quarters of a million miners came out on strike, causing industrial havoc and a further 1 250 000 industrial workers to be forced into idleness. The Government introduced a Bill to set up minimum-wage machinery, similar to the proposals it had made before the strike began. Once the Act was passed, the strike was called off. In his book *England 1870–1914* historian R. C. K. Ensor, discussing the strike, comments:

If the strikes of the previous year had shown the advantages of combination on a large scale, this coal strike illustrated its drawbacks. The Miners' Federation was an unwieldy stiff-jointed body; tied to its voted programme and schedules, it lacked freedom and flexibility to meet opportunity halfway. Moreover, once so large a human mass had been laboriously set in motion towards a strike, nobody could prevent it occurring, even after it had become superfluous. In the result the miners gained a good deal; but they could have had it all before the stoppage.

During the coal strike many firms used their commercial vehicles in efforts to beat the industrial blockade. There was trouble near Leeds when some lorry owners sent their vans to the pit-heads to collect coal, whilst at Bristol reduced railway services due to the strike led to an increased use of commercial vehicles. King George V, H.M. the Queen and Queen Alexandra each sent a cheque for £1000 to the president of the Local Government Board towards the relief of those who had suffered from the coal dispute. On 5th April, the day after the strike ended, *The Times* editorial stated:

The strike was presented to the miners as a great and generous struggle, on behalf not only of themselves but of all workers, to obtain recognition of a principle which would eventually bring great benefits to all. Thus we may understand the apparent callousness to the sufferings of men in other occupations. If we imagine men fighting for what they conceive as a great emancipation for all their fellow workmen as well as for themselves, we can understand that they saw no harm in the other beneficiaries suffering present loss together with themselves. . . .

A week later Britain was stunned by the news that the *Titanic* had sunk after a collision with an iceberg whilst on her maiden voyage.

Less than a month after this disaster a new economic threat to prosperity came with the London Dock dispute which lasted for six weeks. One of the reasons for the eventual failure of the strike was the decision of the L.C.C. that it could not feed the children of striking dockers during the school summer holidays. At the beginning of the strike a convoy, consisting mostly of horse-drawn vehicles, left the Victoria and Albert Docks under a guard of mounted police, to take meat to Smithfield Market. *En route* for Smithfield the convoy was halted by strikers as the horses were attempting to draw their heavy loads of frozen meat up a steep hill. A skirmish ensued and the drivers, disliking the difficulties involved, refused to handle horse traffic on future occasions. Realizing the problems and the seriousness of the situation, the Home Office negotiated with the owners of the S.S. *Highland Brae* and also with the purchasers of the perishable cargo stored in her hold. As a result of the negotiations E. W. Rudd Ltd, a firm of motor-haulage contractors, was employed to transport the cargo from the docks to London where there was a feeling almost amounting to panic that the shortage of supplies would lead to profiteering and vast food prices. Rudd's used a fleet of sixteen steam wagons to carry 150 tons of frozen beef from the docks, with a protection of more than a hundred mounted police. As the convoy left the docks it was jeered by a crowd of sullen and militant dockers. During the journey to Smithfield Market via Commercial Road and Hounds-ditch stones were thrown at the drivers, several of whom suffered minor cuts and bruises where the stones hit their target. Mr E. W. Rudd steered the leading wagon in the first convoy to show his em-ployees that he was prepared to accept the same risks as he expected them to accept. Due to the enterprise of the Rudd convoys, the *Highland Brae* was unloaded almost on time, for four processions of lorries entered and left the docks every twenty-four hours. In an interview Mr Rudd said:

I have no desire to beat down the men, nor to act as a breaker of labour. In my opinion, however, food for the people is of supreme importance, and I consider myself quite justified in going to any lengths to prevent the price of food rising in London. I think that the strikers are mistaken, and as a proof that my actions and general business conduct are not inconsis-tent with these remarks, let me point out that the drivers of my wagons have not registered the slightest protest when called upon to do this haulage during the strike. It is only by using my steamers that I have been able to cope with this extremely heavy work. Five hundred horses would have been of no use to me. I cannot speak too highly of the work which the wagons have performed under exceptional strike conditions. Superinten-dent Wells of Scotland Yard has afforded me the greatest assistance, and he has at all times been ready to fall in with any suggestion that I have made. I may say that during the ordinary working week my firm is res-ponsible for the cartage of 200 tons of beef, and the steam wagons have proved, in this emergency, that they are elastic enough to carry double that amount, and to work for twenty-four hours a day if necessary.

After the strike was over the police made it clear that they could not have coped with transporting the supplies from the docks to the London markets had it not been for the use of the commercial vehicles. Mr Rudd added that it was easier for the police to protect twenty motor vehicles than a pair of horse-drawn vehicles against angry strikers who were not prepared to risk life and limb holding up a steam vehicle which was careeing through the dock gates at a speed of 10 m.p.h.

The year 1913 opened with Britain awaking to the realization that war with Germany was not a remote possibility. Although the Kaiser had visited England in late spring of 1911 for the unveiling of the Queen Victoria Memorial, and the Crown Prince had attended the coronation, the sending of a German gunboat to Agadir had given an indication that relations between Germany and other European countries were strained. Hints were made in newspaper editorials of Germany's lust for further territorial possessions, and also of her increasing military strength. However, in February 1913 the British nation were more perturbed to learn of the death of Captain Scott at the South Pole, and the activities of the Suffragettes under the leadership of Mrs Pankhurst. The day of the horse-drawn omnibus was ending, and by midsummer there were less than a hundred operating in London, as compared with 3500 a decade earlier. In May King George V and Queen Mary, on a visit to the North-West, stayed at Crewe Hall where Lord Crewe had arranged for them to be entertained by the Foden Brass Band during the evening. The King appeared so pleased with the band that they were commanded to perform again the following morning. In conversation with their conductor the King queried the fact that all the musicians were employed at Fodens and practised in their own free time. It was explained to him that they were all members of the factory works force. He then requested that every member of the band should be told of the great pleasure they had given to the royal party.

Life at Foden's Elworth works at this time was arduous. Work began at 6 a.m. and continued until 5.30 p.m., except on Saturday when the works closed at midday. The employees had forty minutes for their breakfast and an hour for lunch. There were no canteen facilities, and the 500 workers brought their own sandwiches, and brewed cans of tea on stoves. Many of the workers lived in houses at Sandbach built for them by the company, whose founder, Edwin Foden, used to walk through the workshops every day. Broad-shouldered, with sideboards, but otherwise clean-shaven, he invariably wore a half tall shiner top hat. A great perfectionist, if he inspected a casting with a little blow-hole in it, he would say to the fitter – all of whom he knew by their Christian names – 'Lend me a hammer', and he would smash the casting, saying as he did so,

'That's got to be melted up. That will never go into a vehicle.' He was a clever and a practical engineer and inventor who became annoyed if he saw a job being done badly. If he saw a fitter doing his task without due skill and craftsmanship he would take the file from him and explain how the task should be done as he tackled it himself. He lived in a house which adjoined the administrative offices of the works and was active in the business until his death in 1911.

The fitter's day usually began with preparing the cylinders and scraping the valves. There were few machine tools, and even fewer jigs. Much of the work was marked out with chalk and scribers. Unemployment was always a threat, and the dreaded voice of the foreman saying, 'If you cannot do better than this, then go home,' made the workers maintain a high standard of efficiency. Once a fitter had completed his seven years' apprenticeship, he was likely to become a machinist, skilled fitter, moulder or foundryman, with his weekly wage increased to twenty-six shillings. The problem was that if trade was bad the company could not afford to keep the fitters unless their work was of an exceptionally high standard. Many workers were compelled to leave after their seven years' training. Apprentices, too, could suffer from the economic depression, and it was in their own interest to stay in favour with the foreman. One of the most disagreeable of their tasks was to crawl into the water tanks of the steamers to clean them. The smell from the red-lead paint made them drowsy, and their companions had to thump on the tank to ensure that they were still awake.

The question of running costs was always prevalent in the minds of commercial vehicle manufacturers and users. In an effort to clarify these costs Leyland produced a comprehensive analysis in their 1913 catalogue pp. 69–76.

One large firm particularly interested in these costs was Sainsburys, who had commenced their commercial vehicle fleet in 1905 with the purchase of two 5-ton Straker Squire steam wagons. These were sold when it was decided to change to petrol-driven vehicles for the reason that petrol-driven vehicles were giving better results. By 1913 Sainsburys had seven Milnes-Daimlers, comprising two 28 h.p. 3½-tonners, four 35 h.p. 4-tonners, and one 35 h.p. 5-tonner. The drivers for these vehicles had been obtained from Milnes-Daimler at the same time as the vehicles were purchased, for Sainsburys did not believe in attempting to teach the drivers of horse-drawn wagons the intricacies of mechanical transport. The vehicles had a petrol consumption of seven miles to the gallon, and averaged 20 000 miles per set of tyres.

Continued on p. 77.

LEYLAND MOTORS LIMITED (1913)

A FEW INTERESTING DETAILS ON 'COSTS'

What people want to know when they first consider purchase of Commercial Vehicles, is —

1. The Prime Cost? And, having decided to face the capital outlay,
2. What will they cost to *run*?
3. Shall they be *steam* or *petrol*?
4. Shall they be *rubber* or *steel* tyred?
5. What nett profit will they make above the cost of rail or horse transport?

The above are all vital questions to the prospective owner. In this short article we discuss these various methods of transport to help him to arrive at a decision.

Prime Cost   1. The prime cost of Steam Wagons is on page 16, Petrol Chassis on page 30. Special bodies, etc., under the various sections.

Running Costs   2. The answer is given very fully on pages 14 and 15, where the costs are worked out fairly and under average conditions. The rates per year, per week, per day, per mile, and per ton-mile are all given, and even for ton-mileage when loaded one and both ways. All that is necessary is to decide on the carrying capacity required, and then refer to the heading under this size, and costs are given in detail for mileages of 40, 60, 80, and 100 per day. Heavy bodies, such as Vans, etc., must be considered partly as load carried. In these tables the body is assumed to be a plain platform, and as such is *not* included in the *load*, which is therefore nett. Thus, if a 3-ton motor is decided on the 3 tons can be carried on a plain platform. But only about 2¾ to 2¼ tons in a van body.

Steam v. Petrol   3. This question requires a careful consideration of circumstances, depending greatly on mileage, loads, local conditions, terminal delays, and so on. It is really best to consult us directly on the matter. We always have the customer's interests at heart, and especially as we make both *steam* and *petrol* lorries we can advise you. As a general rule, however, *steam* is better for *short mileages* and *big loads*, especially where a trailer is employed and the loads get up to 8, 10, and even to 12 tons. For *long mileages* and *small loads* the *petrol* lorry is better, as it goes at a greater speed than the steamer, viz., 12 miles per hour as against 5 miles per hour. Take examples of the two cases.

Steam

Take first, a steam wagon and trailer loaded *both* ways with 10 tons and a mileage of 20 miles out and the same back. The ton-mileage is 400, and the cost on macadam roads (which are more severe by a long way than setts), is £8 per week, see page 15, column 42. This comes out at 32/- per day or $\frac{32/-}{40\ miles} = 9\frac{1}{2}$d. per mile.

or 1d. per ton of load per mile carried. These conditions are the best that can be got out of a steam wagon. Loaded *one* way only the ton-mileage is just about 10% less than double, or 1·8d. per ton per mile, or say 2d. at the very outside. The conditions in general town work are easier, and the costs come nearer 25/- per day, or if three loads are obtained = 30 tons (loaded one way) *the cost per ton* = 10d. for a haul of say four miles, on the average. This has even been improved with a 12-ton load, and four journeys or 48 tons (such cases are common on an organised collection and delivery) to 6¼d. per ton hauled. On work like this a *petrol motor* cannot hope to compete. So one asks where then does a petrol motor come in? The answer is: when mileages of 50, 60, 80, or 100 are tackled in the day. A steam wagon cannot do this, since it only travels at 5 miles per hour, as already stated. The petrol does 12 miles per hour, *i.e.* 2½ to 3 times the speed, but *without* a trailer. A case in point is a railway rate of 12/- per ton and loads of 5 tons (say) *both* ways. Take page 14, column 6, for a 5-tonner at 60 miles per day, and you get total cost at 49/- per day or 5/- per ton, or loaded *one way*, 9/6 per ton. This shows a saving of not less than 2/6 per ton, or £3 2 6 per week, or £156 per annum. Generally, loads are obtained both ways, showing a saving of 7/- per ton, or £17 10 0 per week, or £875 per year, as it is called, 'paying for the motor the first year'.

Tyres

4.   The question of tyres is also important. Petrol motors in this country seldom or never run on steel tyres, rubber being the best for high speeds. Steam wagons are sometimes run on rubber tyres, but in 90% of the cases steel is the cheaper. It is not that rubber would not *suit* steam wagons, but because the price paid is next door to prohibitive. Let us explain this. The steam wagon is very heavy in itself. It tares 5 tons without,

Tare

water, fuel, oil, or men. Add a tank full of water to that in the boiler, several cwts. of coke or coal, oil, men, etc., and the tare (unladen) comes up to nearly 6½ tons dead weight. Now put a load of 5½ tons on, which brings the gross load up to the 12-ton legal limit, and you have 8 tons on the back axle and 4 tons on the front axle with an evenly-distributed load. You now see why the fitting of rubber tyres is 'barred' on steamers.

Speed

The legal speed (on rubber) goes up to 8 miles per hour, but remember the law does not allow you a trailer at the higher speed, and so you lose the best paying part of the load. There are a few exceptions where a steam vehicle may pay on rubbers, but they are not of such general importance to be considered by the average user.

Snow

One of these conditions is snow, as the steel-shod tyre cannot be used with success. But the percentages of days stopped for this reason do not warrant the heavy expenditure (about £250) for rubber tyres and spare wheels.

Now take a problem, which is receiving a certain amount of consideration at present, due to the temporarily high price of petrol – we refer to the 3-ton steamer on rubbers and supposed to travel at 12 miles per hour. We refer you to costs under columns 45 and 46 on page 15. Compare same with 3-ton petrol costs under Columns 13 and 15 on page 14. A glance shows you that the steamer cannot compare at all favourably; in fact, we may state that up till recently we made a 3-ton steamer ourselves and found we *had no sale for* same in competition with our own make of 3-ton petrol. The reasons are obvious – the tare of the 'light'

steamer is just about 10-cwts. less than the 5 and 6-ton steamer, and comes out at 6 tons dead unladen. Granted (at the present price of petrol) a saving is shown on the steamer fuel, but look at the price of the tyres. And the steamer requires two men always, and is more or less dirty, and takes about one hour to get up steam. It has to pick water about every 15 miles, and can only carry a limited amount of coke or coal. The

petrol is *always* ready to start, is clean, has a tare unladed of $3\frac{1}{4}$ tons only, and carries fuel for 160 miles or so in a small tank under the driver's seat. So convinced are we of the advantages offered by the 3-ton petrol that, as stated, we quite recently ceased to manufacture the 3-ton steamer. Our opinion is *unbiassed* too, as we are makers of both types – steam, 5 tons and upwards, and petrol, all sizes from 6 tons down to 15-cwts.

5. Let us now compare cartage by horses. To be fair in both cases (motor and horses) all charges are to be included.

Take the case of a 2-horse lorry complete:

Capital Outlay

2 horses at £60 each	..	£120 0 0
2 sets harness at £20 per set	..	40 0 0
1 lorry	..	30 0 0
		£190 0 0

Annual Expenditure

Interest at 5% on £190	..	..	£9 10 0
Depreciation, horses, 10%	..	..	12 0 0
,, lorry, 10%	..	..	3 0 0
,, harness, 10%	..	..	4 0 0
Fodder, at 13/6 per week	..	..	66 0 0
Stables, at £10 per year per horse	..	..	20 0 0
Harness and repairs	..	..	4 0 0
Vet.'s charges, £1 10 0 per horse	..	..	3 0 0
Farriery, £3 10 0 per horse	..	..	7 0 0
Carter, at 35/- per week	..	..	91 0 0
Insurance, $2\frac{1}{2}$%	..	..	5 0 0
			£224 10 0

This shows that a team lorry costs (say) £230 per annum, or £4 12 0 per week, or 18/- per day. Take the average mileage at 18 per day, and the average load at 4 tons. This gives a rate of 1/- per mile, or loaded *both* ways, 3d. per ton per mile, or loaded *one* way, 5·4d. per ton per mile. (Average speed of horse, 3 miles per hour.)

Petrol v. Horse

Now to compare motors with above, let us take two examples – 'A' petrol, and 'B' steam. The petrol motor averages 12 miles per hour, and carries (say) 4 tons on a mileage (say) of 60. The steam motor averages 5 miles per hour, and carries 6 tons, or 10 tons on (say) 18 miles.

'A' Costs of 4-ton PETROL Motor from table
(80 miles per day)

1 motor, as per costs under column 10, page 14.
£656 per annum as cost for 80 miles per day.
Or £13 2 0 per week of 5 days.
Or £2 12 6 per day.

Costs of 8 Horses and 4 Lorries
(18 miles)

8 horses and 4 lorries as per detailed costs.
£910 per annum at 18 miles per day.
Or £18 per week.
Or £3 12 0 per day.

Assume length of journey 10 miles out and same back (approximately)

Description		1 Motor	2 Horses	8 Horses
Time travelling	:	1¼ hours	10¼ hours	10¼ hours
„ loading and unloading	:	1⅜ hours	1⅜ hours	1⅜ hours
In 12 hours	:	4 journeys	1 journey	—
„	:	4 journeys	—	4 journeys
„	:	16 tons	4 tons	16 tons
„	:	3/4½ per ton	4/6 per ton	4/6 per ton

'B' Costs of 6-ton STEAM Wagon from table
1 motor as per cost under Columns 41 and 42
£400 per annum as cost for 36 miles per day.
Or £8 per week of 5 days.
Or £1 12 0 per day.

Costs of 4 horses and 2 lorries (18 miles)
4 horses and 2 lorries as per detailed costs.
£455 per annum.
Or £9 per week.
Or £1 16 0 per day.

Assume length of journey again at 3 miles out and same back

Description	1 Motor	1 Motor and Trailer (10 tons)	2 Horses	4 Horses	6 Horses
Time travelling	1 hour	1 hour	2 hours	2 hours	2 hours
„ loading and unloading	1¼ hours	1¼ hours	1 hour	1 hour	1 hour
In 9 hours	4 journeys	4 journeys	3 journeys	—	—
„	4 journeys	4 journeys	—	6 journeys	9 journeys
„	24 tons	40 tons	12 tons	24 tons	36 tons
„	1/3 per ton	9½d. per ton	1/6 per ton	1/6 per ton	1/6 per ton

These two cases are instructive, as they show at once that on the short mileages, where *horses* still are in favour, that one petrol lorry will do the same tonnage as 8 horses at a less rate per ton. The capital outlay on the petrol (4-tonner) is about £760, and on the petrol (4-tonner) is about £760, and on 8 horses and 4 lorries the very same.

Now in the case of the 6-ton steam wagon the results are also better than horses. Without a trailer 4 horses are displaced for a similar tonnage, and work done at 3d. per ton less; but with a trailer and a 10-ton load more than 6 horses are displaced and the cost per ton reduced 50%. The advantage therefore of *short* mileages and *large* tonnages are all in favour of the steam wagon. Capital outlay for steamer £550, and for 6 horses and 3 lorries, £570. This, we want you to note, does not by any means prove that the petrol is outdone either by horses or steam wagons; it simply means that the short mileage added to the delays in loading and unloading are not suitable for a fast vehicle. To prove this one has only to take an *actual* case in point. Again we take the 4-ton petrol and load it *one* way first, and give it a straight run of 30 miles out and 30 miles back – total 60 miles. Refer to costs sheets (Column 10), and you will see that £2 3 0 per day covers all the costs.

Railway

The rate per ton is therefore 10/9 and the railway rate is 13/– per ton, saving 2/3 per ton loaded one way. But a return load is almost always found, and so the results *actually* are 8 tons at 13/– per ton = 104/– per day. Motor costs, £2 3 0 per day. So saving is 61/– or £3 per day or £15 per week, or £750 per annum; or, as already stated, the motor 'pays for itself in a year'. Result: Long mileage and loaded both ways show a very large saving by petrol motor over horse, railway, or steam wagon.

Relief for Congestion

One final word re motors. A great deal of congestion at present exists in Railway Goods Stations, Docks, Warehouses, etc., which causes serious delays in loading and unloading and in getting loads at all. Does it not, therefore, stand to reason that motors will reduce this congestion? Why? Because one motor does away with 4, 6, 8, or more horses for the same tonnage moved, and so the fewer number of vehicles are about at one time to get in one another's way. Think this article carefully over, and write us for further information.

"LEYLAND" MOTORS – TYRE DEPARTMENT

Guarantee

We can guarantee the tyres sold on "Leyland" Chassis for 10,000 miles, or so much of that as has been run within the first 12 months from the date of fitting, provided the vehicle is not overloaded or overrun, and that it is confined to proper roads and yards in reasonably good repair, and remains in the United Kingdom.

Allowance

In the event of the first set of tyres, complying with the above restrictions, failing before they have accomplished the 10,000 miles, or within the 12 months, an amount representing a proper proportion of the sale price of the tyre, equal to the unfinished mileage or unexpired months as the case may be, will be credited off the invoice, for the new tyre, *e.g.*, if the new set are to cost £100 and the old set have only done 5,000 miles, the credit would be £50; or if the mileage is small and the tyres are charged at the end of the 10th month, two months, *i.e.*, two-twelfths of their price will be credited. The allowance is to be calculated by time or distance at our option.

In the unlikely event of the second set being unsatisfactory, we give you the option of changing the make to that of any other tyre on our list, when we will still credit the unexpired mileage of the old set off the new brand of tyre.

Regulations

The following conditions must be rigidly observed to obtain our rebates:—

1. A suitable journey book must be kept and entered up daily.
2. A diary must be kept when each tyre is put on and taken off, the tyres being known by numbers.
3. One of our postcard summaries must be completed and sent to us for each vehicle each week.

Inspection

4. The books must be available to our inspectors at your Offices in working hours, and you must undertake to explain, satisfactorily, how the mileage is calculated.

5. When tyres are to be replaced you must communicate with us as to whether the work is to be done at our Works or locally.

6. Serious damage should be reported to give us a chance of making a temporary repair if we think it necessary.

Makes

The following Manufacturers are under Contract with us, and current prices for any of their tyres will be sent on application.

"LEYLAND" PRIVATE CODE

The following Code (Copyright) may be found useful.

	Code Word	
ENQUIRIES	Acafee	Please quote your present price for another ....motor(s), similar to the last supplied.
	Acafic	Please say if you have in stock, or how soon you can deliver, and lowest price, for............
	Acaflo	Please telephone or telegraph us at our expense by what train goods are sent.
	Acafov	Please write giving us full particulars.
	Acaful	Please wire cost of alterations proposed.
	Acafyv	We are waiting reply to our letter (or wire) of............
	Acagag	Have you sent remittance? if so, when? and how?
	Acagel	Can you recommend a good driver?
ORDERS	Acagib	Please send by passenger train.
	Acagof	Please send by parcel post.
	Acagun	Please send by goods express, labelled "Urgent".
	Acagyf	Please instruct your representative to call upon us.
	Acahak	Please accept the instructions of our driver.
	Acaheb	Our motor requires overhauling. Please examine it on arrival and wire us approximate cost and time required.
	Acahig	Your tender is accepted, please proceed with the work.

Acahoe		Please telegraph credit and instruct your Bankers to advise us that documents are to be negotiated when presented.
Acahuf		Send a supply of catalogues.
Acahyb		Send a price list of parts.
Acajal		Please send us an expert driver for ....
Acajed		Send a set of tyres as supplied with the motor originally.
Acajim		Please send man at our expense to examine and report on our motor.
Acajoc		Please send men at once to repair our motor, and bring ....
Acajug		Our motor is broken down at .... Please send to bring it home at our expense. Will unload and meet your men .... station. Wire time of arrival ....
Acakam		Our motor is broken down at .... Please send to take it to your works at our expense. Will unload and meet your men at .... station.
Acaken	**ADVICE**	We very strongly recommend.
Acakip		Prices are now advanced.
Acakog		Prices are now reduced.
Acakur		Our terms are one-third with the order and balance when motor is ready at our works.
Acakye		Terms for Export. One-third with order and balance in England against shipping documents.
Acalak		Shipment has been delayed through congested traffic on railway.
Acalea		We have the B/L and are awaiting instructions from your Bankers.
Acalif		Vehicle packed ready for boat.
Acalon		Bankers have no authority to negotiate documents.
Acalum		We shipped last week.
Acalyk		We shipped last month.
Acamap		We are shipping this week.
Acamek		We are shipping this month.
Acamia		We are shipping next week.
Acamoo		We are shipping next month.
Acamus		In reply to your letter (or wire) of ....
Acamya		Please refer to your letter (or wire) of ....
Acanar		Please refer to our letter (or wire) of ....
Acanem		Your Motor will be on test probably in .... days.
Acanil		Your motor will be on test this week.
Acanop		Your motor will be on test to-morrow.

The battle of steam versus petrol lasted until 1914, by which time the petrol engine was supreme for use in the lighter classes of vehicles although it could not compete with the power and reliability of the steam engine for heavy lorries. Throughout the first decade of the century manufacturers of steam wagons made many improvements to the efficiency of their locomotives. By 1908 proposals were being put forward to use rubber in place of steel as tyres for self-contained steam wagons, and two years later steam-wagon builders had produced a lighter type of machine with rubber tyres for loads of three tons. These new machines were considered a challenge to petrol vehicles for goods carrying. In 1912 the steady increase in the price of petrol, upon which a tax of 3d a gallon had been introduced in 1909, caused a further demand for steam vehicles. Statistics showed that the costs of running a steam vehicle were 7d per mile for a weekly total of 300 miles for a 3½-tonner and 10·1 pence per mile for 5-tonners on a 200 mile per week basis. At the outbreak of the war the military authorities did not look favourably upon steam wagons, although in October 1914 twenty-five 5-ton Fodens and trailers were ordered. Scarcity of petrol resulted in an increased demand for 3-ton steam wagons for use at home during the war years and there is little doubt that there was justification for their description as 'a national asset'. In 1915 the Sentinel Co. – one of the biggest of the steam-wagon builders – moved from Glasgow to Shrewsbury. At a later date the chairman of Sentinel claimed that the steam wagon formed the cheapest, quickest and most reliable means of transporting loads from three tons to ten tons over distances up to 100 miles. He added that the use of coal-using wagons in Britain reduced the petrol imports by more than £1 000 000 a year.

For years diplomatic correspondents, members of the Foreign Office, politicians and industrialists had warned the nation of Germany's mood of aggression. Despite such warnings the War Office had been dilatory, and had only been prodded from its lethargy by the efforts of others. In an attempt to prove the usefulness of transporting soldiers by means of mechanical vehicles, the secretary of the Automobile Association, Mr Stenson Cooke, had organized a company of guards and their equipment to be transported from their London depot to Hastings and back in the same day by a fleet of twenty-one taxicabs, five motor buses and two 3-ton lorries. Nearly eighteen months elapsed after this memorable trip which took place on 17th March 1909 before commercial vehicles were used in army manoeuvres. Even then the military authorities concentrated on the use of tractors despite news from Germany and France that self-contained vehicles had proved more efficient. By 1912 some progress had been made and the British Army had fifteen military mechanical transport companies, many of which took part in the manoeuvres held during the year. During one manoeuvre more than a hundred vehicles were involved – the Blue Force using petrol-driven vehicles and the Red Force using both petrol and steam vehicles. The military judges considered that the petrol vehicles had proved the better. In December 1912 it was proposed that a sum of £1 400 000 be spent on the purchase of motor lorries which should be used for commercial transport work through the medium of a government-controlled company. Little or nothing came of the proposal. In the meantime private enterprise was showing great initiative and Waring and Gillow created from their fleet of motor lorries a Mechanical Transport Reserve of four vehicles, a superintendent, forty-two men and 110 cadets. When war was declared this contingent was pressed into service within twenty hours, as were fleets of vehicles owned by Carter Paterson. For the most part when war was declared vehicles that were commandeered were taken over at cost price less 15 per cent for each year that the vehicle had been in use.

In the summer of 1914 the majority of Englishmen were stubbornly oblivious to the gathering war clouds. In April King George V had made history by becoming the first monarch to attend a cup final when he watched Burnley play Liverpool at the Crystal Palace, and in London sophisticated men about town hummed the words

> I'm Gilbert the Filbert
> The Knut with a 'K'
> The pride of Piccadilly
> The blasé roue.

Charlie Chaplin was taking the film world by storm, petrol was a shilling a gallon, and a suffragette broke the glass panels of a cabinet in the Asiatic Room of the British Museum. At the seaside a popular song included the verse

> Then he'd get back at the wheel
> A dozen times they'd start to hug and kiss –
> And then the darned old engine it would miss,
> And then he'd have to get under,
> Get out and get under
> And fix up his automobile!

Whilst thousands of holiday-makers hummed and sang this music-hall ditty two young Sandbach boys, Reg and Ted Foden, were finding their fun by starting up the steam wagons which were housed in a large garage at the Elworth works during the weekend. The snag with this otherwise harmless prank was that once started the boys could not stop their fiery steeds which on more than one occasion

smashed through the garage doors. The culprits were suitably punished by their father!

On the morning of Tuesday, 4th August, the Prime Minister told the House of Commons that an ultimatum had been given to the German Government, and that it expired at midnight. When the message was sent out by the Admiralty the following morning to all His Majesty's ships: 'Commence hostilities against Germany', few thought that the war would last more than a month. There was a sense of optimism as Britain girded her loins for action, and a young officer's happy remark, 'Isn't it lucky that I have been born so that I am just the right age and in just the right place?' was a typical example of the outlook towards the war. Another view which was less patriotic was that of a cavalry officer who expressed the hope that whilst he was in France the farmers would maintain the country-side, for he was afraid that otherwise 'we'll come back to some pretty bloody hunting this winter'.

In the first weeks of the war Sir John Dickinson, sitting at Bow Street, had been actively engaged in signing warrants authorizing the military authorities to requisition motors needed for the war effort. Each warrant was put into operation by two military officers accompanied by a police sergeant. Some motor-vehicle owners were unamused by the loss of their vehicles, and a Manchester charabanc owner had his vehicle seized less than a day after he had bought and paid for it. Employees from Fodens, Thornycroft, Milnes-Daimler and Garretts were amongst those who joined the colours within a week of the declaration of war, and the Commercial Motor Users Association placed its entire organization at the disposal of the War Office. By the end of August commercial vehicles of every British make had found their way to Paris where they were under the direction of the Army Service Corps. Spare parts had been shipped across the Channel and mechanics could be seen making necessary repairs at the side of the boulevards. The two most common faults to be repaired were cracked cylinders, and broken axles caused by too little ground clearance over the *pavé* of the French roads. Some vehicles had been commandeered direct from the manufacturers whilst others had been compulsorily acquired under the War Office subsidized vehicles scheme.

During 1912 the War Office had held subsidized Vehicle Trials to determine which vehicles in two classes, 30 cwt and 3 ton, would be accepted as qualifying for the subsidy scheme. Owners of qualified vehicles could enrol them and receive for each vehicle a purchase premium of £50 and an annual subsidy of £20 for three years. The one obligation was to maintain the vehicle to the satisfaction of the War Department inspectors. At any time the Army Reserve was called out, the War Department were entitled to purchase the vehicles at their existing value, plus 25 per cent – the owners being compelled to effect delivery within seventy-two hours. When the Trials took place Leyland entered two vehicles, one in each class. These vehicles, the only ones to be awarded certificates, proved so satisfactory from the military viewpoint that between April 1912 and April 1913 the War Office ordered eighty-eight similar vehicles.

Many of the lorries used to transport ammunition to the troops preparing to fight the Battle of Tours were brand-new Daimlers which had been driven direct from the factory to the point of embarkation, and from thence across the Channel before being loaded and redirected to the front. One fact which became apparent immediately was that chaos could ensue if the vehicles in each convoy were not of the same type. Unless this was enforced the problems of climbing hills could become complex with some lorries able to carry their loads to the top without any difficulty or undue effort, whilst others laboured to do so in vain. There were times when heavy lorries with the name of the furniture maker to whom they belonged still emblazoned on the panelling, struggled to drag a heavy gun to the brow of a hill, whilst light vans towing searchlights in their wake found no problem in climbing the same hill if they could pass the lorry! The French army authorities planned that where possible the lorries should be fitted out to enable them to fulfil a dual purpose; firstly, to carry provisions and ammunition to the troops at the front, and on their return journey to base to carry out the second purpose of transporting the wounded to the casualty hospitals. Whenever possible the lorries were supplied with a canvas cover supported on hoops which would allow hammocks to be slung on them for the comfort of the wounded. For many of the drivers the new conditions seemed fun after the humdrum existence of acting as delivery agents in peacetime Britain, with narrow escapes from death after being challenged at night by inexperienced trigger-happy sentries, being shelled by the enemy and fêted by the French villagers. By October, many of them would have gladly returned to their previous humdrum existence. The German armies, retreating after the Battle of the Marne, were leaving the countryside little more than a barren wasteland. The majority of the roads, described as 'chemins de grande communication' and 'chemins vicineaux', were narrow and only lightly surfaced. In consequence the drivers found conditions deplorable, with the verges on either side of the road nothing more than a sea of mud into which their vehicles frequently sank. Fears were expressed that when the winter set in the British lorries, with inadequate ground clearance, would fail to cope with these conditions. Straw, sacking and ropes were always carried to assist when skidding tyres failed to get a grip on the road surface, but nevertheless hours were wasted almost every day in dragging lorries from ditches. The great excitement of each day was the capture of German vehicles, or the collection of those abandoned by the fleeing enemy at the side of the road. The usual German practice when abandoning a lorry was to remove the front wheels, steering wheel, magneto and water-pipe connections, and to damage the radiator and petrol tank. The British drivers had no difficulties over the supplies of petrol even though they were unable to acquire any from the French authorities, for the War Office had arranged for virtually limitless supplies, in two-gallon tins, to be shipped across the Channel.

At home, the first six months of the war found the commercial vehicle industry beset by many problems. There was a consensus of opinion that the quality and capabilities of British-manufactured lorries had played an important part in the establishment of the British forces in France, but there was concern as to future output. Many engineering firms, depleted by members of the staff joining the forces, were being ordered to manufacture munitions instead of components for commercial vehicles. With commercial vehicle production in the doldrums, American manufacturers were attempting to establish themselves in the British market. The Government, conservative in their outlook as to the manufacture of vehicles, placed most of their orders with the established firms – much to the chagrin of men such as Herbert Austin. However, by the autumn of 1915 Austin were making shells, trucks, guns, ambulances and armoured cars. Women were employed at Longbridge for the first time, and housing for employees became so great a problem that Austin ordered sectional wooden bungalows from America. Unfortunately, although the side walls arrived safely, the roofs had been shipped aboard the ill-fated *Lusitania*. A consignment of Austin vehicles was shipped to Russia, and Herbert Austin was horrified to learn that the Russian peasants who were assembling the trucks put the gearbox grease on their bread instead of butter! At Cowley, the Morris factory, geared to assemble motor-car components, changed to the manufacture of hand grenades and mine sinkers.

In the years immediately preceding the war, classes had been instituted at Leylands to train officers of the Army Service Corps in mechanical transport. When the war started, much of Leyland's output was on behalf of the A.S.C., with the Royal Flying Corps also demanding a number of the 3-ton models powered by the 32 h.p. four-cylinder engine. As the demands of the Flying Corps became greater as the duration of the war lengthened, it was decided that Leylands should have their entire output allocated to the Flying Corps which became the Royal Air Force in 1918. During the war years Leylands produced more than 5400 vehicles for the Air Force, the majority of them being the famous R.A.F. type which took a driver, armed guard and a party of air mechanics in the main part of the body, the rear part being sheeted in to give weather-proof accommodation for breakdown work and room for spares and replacement parts. Leyland also produced travelling workshops, with the vehicles fitted with special bodies which opened out all round to form platforms and canopies. These lorries carried a full range of workshop equipment, including a petrol electric generating and lighting set which provided power for electrically driven lathes and other equipment. Like many other commercial vehicle firms, the war years found the production at Leyland vastly increased. By 1918 the output had been trebled, and their payroll doubled, with the ensuing large-scale land purchases, factory extensions and additions to plant.

Another commercial vehicle company which was transformed by the war was A.E.C., which had been founded in 1906 as the Vanguard Company at a small factory in Walthamstow. By 1912 their 'B' type, powered by a 30 h.p. petrol engine, was known to all Londoners who used open-topped double-decker buses. So reliable did these 'B' types prove that during the war more than 1300 of them were acquired by the War Office for service in France whilst another 300 were employed in defence work in London. The War Department also ordered more than 10000 of A.E.C.'s 'Y' type 3–4-ton trucks which were built for military transport duties. The production of these vehicles, powered by a 45 h.p. petrol engine, necessitated a moving-track assembly line which was almost unique at the time, and which produced one lorry every half-hour of the day. As the war dragged on interminably, commercial vehicles played their part in every sphere of operations. The roughest war service for vehicles was in the Caucasus and the Balkans where Lanchesters were used as armoured cars. However, it was the use of tanks at the Battle of the Somme which brought the greatest contribution of commercial vehicles to the Allied victory.

In the late spring of 1916 thirty-one-year-old Harry Ricardo was taken to the headquarters of Squadron 20 of the Royal Naval Air Service, based in a Pall Mall office, sworn to secrecy and shown drawings and photographs of their latest Mark IV tank. His technical advice was needed as to how these 28-ton monsters could be placed in position on a specially designed railway truck which was only a few inches wider than the tank. Ricardo helped to solve this problem and many other of the teething troubles of the first tanks which had been conceived in the final months of 1914. At the instigation of Winston Churchill the R.N.A.S. had been formed from civilian technical engineers who had volunteered, and had been divided into a number of independent squadrons each commanded by a naval engineering officer. Squadron 20 had been allocated the task of developing an armoured vehicle capable of crossing wide trenches and of driving its way through barbed wire. Both Churchill and Lloyd George showed the greatest enthusiasm for the project, but their enthusiasm was not shared by those generals who were still convinced that the war would be won by the superior use of cavalry.

Once the project was evolved, a committee under the chairmanship of the Director of Naval Construction was formed and began to design H.M. Landships, the prototypes for which were built by Messrs Foster of Lincoln under their chief engineer William Tritton. A most energetic member of the committee was Sir Albert Stern, one of the wealthiest bankers in the country, but even he had difficulty in persuading the military authorities that the project was not the brainchild of eccentric crackpots. Eventually the physical identity of H.M. Landships could be hidden no longer, for more tests were needed whilst as much secrecy as possible was retained. Consequently someone hit upon the notion that the new monster vehicles should be explained as mobile water tanks for use by front-line troops. In this manner was the word 'tank' evolved.

When the military leaders witnessed tank tests at Wolverhampton on ground which had been prepared to resemble conditions in 'no man's land', they were impressed, but insisted that only under real conditions in the front line would the new machines prove or disprove their worth. More than twenty tanks were immediately sent to France, manned by members of Squadron 20 who had little if any experience of the battle front. Within days of their arrival they were ordered to the front, and instructed to cross no man's land, knock out any enemy machine-gun posts, straddle the German trenches, and then ... But there was no further definite command. The entire operation was a haphazard muddle, with virtually no support from infantry who had little idea of what was happening. Once no man's land was crossed some of the tanks pressed farther behind the German lines until they ran out of petrol. Their crews were captured and the German technical engineers were able to examine the tanks at leisure. Other tank crews decided to return intact to the British lines after having reached the enemy front lines. On their return they were able to report not only on the comparative ease with which they had been able to smash through the German defences, but also state a number of faults that they had found when the tanks were in action. They pointed out that larger fuel tanks were needed, and greater stores of ammunition should be carried. Most important, the crews were critical of the 105 h.p. Daimler sleeve-valve engines which had been fitted into the tanks since they were the highest-powered petrol engines available at the time. The engines were not powerful enough to cope with the difficult conditions caused by wallowing in Flanders mud and German barbed wire, and for technical reasons the amount of oil carried into the exhaust port and emitted in a vast cloud of blue smoke made camouflage virtually impossible. In consequence it was decided that an entirely new engine would have to be designed and built.

Various commercial firms such as Mirrlees and Crossley were willing to build the new engine but were reluctant to design it on the grounds that they had insufficient experience. Harry Ricardo was invited to prepare designs for the development of the engine, and was encouraged by Lloyd George, who had become Minister of Munitions early in 1916. A few days before Christmas 1916 Lloyd George told Ricardo that he was intending to order 1400 of the new Mark V tank – even though the design was still on the drawing-board! By midsummer 1917 Mirrlees and Crossley, together with other manufacturers, including Peter Brotherhood, Hornsby, and Bickerton and Day, who had been brought into the group, were producing forty engines a week. One defect of the new engines was that there was too much exhaust pipe inside the hull and the heat became intolerable. This was overcome by installing a sheet metal cowling around the exhaust manifold. Another problem overcome by Ricardo was the danger of engine stalling – never advisable in the middle of no man's land! Before the end of 1917 the tank, now in production at the rate of a hundred a week, was recognized and accepted by the military authorities and the Royal Tank Corps founded. The Germans, taking counter-measures, had developed armour-piercing bullets, which necessitated increasing the thickness of the armour plating. This added to the weight of the tank, and Ricardo felt it was necessary to provide an even more powerful engine. Within months he had perfected a 225 h.p. engine which proved extremely successful. It needs little imagination to appreciate the genius of Ricardo* and the contribution that he made to the Allied victory.

The war ended on 11th November 1918. British soldiers who had dreamed of returning to a land of milk and honey as they lay in the mud of Flanders, came home to find little more than disillusionment. They had hoped for speedy demobilization, a suit of civilian clothes, recognition in the form of war medals and a life of peace in dear old Blighty. Instead they discovered that the spectre of unemployment haunted the streets of every city, as Britain attempted to stabilize her post-war economy. Neutral countries whose production had developed during the war years prospered as the war-ravaged countries of

* Ricardo died in May 1974 aged eighty-nine.

Europe struggled to regain their feet. When King George V sent a message to his people in reply to addresses from the Houses of Lords and Commons a week after the Armistice he wrote: 'Now that the clouds of war are being swept away from the sky, new tasks arise before us. We see more clearly some duties that have been neglected, some weaknesses that may retard our onward march. Liberal provision must be made for those whose exertions by land and sea have saved us. We have to create a better Britain, to bestow more care on the health and well-being of the people, and to ameliorate further the condition of labour.'

Where the commercial vehicle industry was concerned the immediate problem in the post-war period was the disposal of war-worn vehicles. At the end of previous wars the Government of the day had sold off surplus war stores by auction, and these were bought up by syndicates of financiers who retailed them without the slightest regard to the consequences that their actions might have on the reputations of the manufacturers. Many of the leading manufacturers, determined that such a state of affairs should not exist in 1919, put forward proposals to the Reconstruction Committee which had been created for the interest of the Government, the manufacturer and the potential user. The proposals suggested that arrangements should be made whereby manufacturers should be used as a clearing house for the disposal to the public of their respective makes of war service vehicles. The obvious intention behind the proposals was to enable the vehicles to be overhauled and repaired by workmen experienced in the manufacture of particular chassis. Leyland was one of the companies which paid especial attention to this problem. They bought up every one of their war service vehicles which could be traced, including a large batch of lorries parked at St Omer in northern France, and more than forty mobile workshops. These purchases cost in the region of £500000, plus another £225000 for the Sopwith aircraft factory at Kingston where many of the vehicles were sent for reconditioning. About 3000 lorries were recovered and reconditioned, but Leyland did not purchase the Government stock of Leyland spare parts which consequently fell into the unscrupulous hands of others when auctioned by the Government, and were pirated throughout the industry. Many of the purchases made by Leyland came at a moment when their liquid cash position was far from healthy. Young Henry Spurrier III, after returning from the war, became chairman in 1918, and had been advised by financier Clarence Hatry that it would be beneficial to change the name of the company from Leyland Motors (1914) Ltd to Leyland Motors Ltd in order that a new issue of stock could be raised without resorting to Treasury permission. An unforeseen consequence of the changing of the name of the company was that the Government refused to remit to Leylands a proportion of the wartime taxes that they had paid. Such taxes were being refunded to some commercial vehicle manufacturers as a concession according to the amount of their war effort. From Leylands' viewpoint the failure to gain the remission was unfortunate for they were acutely short of ready cash in the early 1920s, and it was not until Aylmer Liardet became general manager that their financial state of affairs moved into calmer waters.

In February 1918 one of the joint managing directors of the Albion Motorcar Co. of Glasgow had been asked his opinion on the motor trade's position on the conclusion of hostilities. He made it clear that he believed that the chief problem would be the disposal of war-worn vehicles. He stated:

In the past the Government simply sold off all surplus war stores by auction, and these were bought up by syndicates who retailed them without the slightest regard to the consequences that their action might have on the reputation of any of the manufacturers. If the same policy is adopted at the end of this war it will lead to serious trouble. The motor manufacturers have a reputation to guard, and they will take whatever steps they think necessary to protect their interests. The question has been, and is being, very carefully considered by the manufacturers and they have laid a scheme before the Government which has been promised sympathetic consideration by the Reconstruction Committee.

In the same interview the Albion director was asked his views as to whether or not the war had done anything to alter the theories of the manufacturers about the design of commercial vehicles. He replied:

The war has certainly taught us many lessons but on the whole we have found that the pre-war design and construction has been substantially correct. So far as Albion is concerned we have made a few minor alterations but nothing has occurred seriously to alter our views as to what was a proper design for a motor vehicle for commercial purposes. As I look to the future I believe that the outlook for the industrial and commercial car is very bright indeed. Take the attitude of the railways, for instance. Hitherto the railway companies have merely nibbled at motor traction, but from personal knowledge and judging by the many enquiries received by our company it is evident that the railway companies are now convinced that motor traction must be developed to an extent hitherto unthought of by them. Motors will be used as feeders for the railways all over the country. No longer will the railway precede the road, but the road will precede the railway . . . horse transport in the big cities will also be largely superseded, and this in itself will mean a great demand for powerful motor vehicles . . . the serious shortage in the supply of suitable horses has compelled many municipalities, hitherto opposed to motor traction, to give it a trial, and they realise that, but for the motor they could not have carried on at all. More and more municipalities will utilize the motor vehicle.

Amongst the post-war problems was that of labour, with many returning ex-servicemen finding it difficult to adapt themselves to the conditions of 'civvy street'. In the Leyland house magazine *Torque* their labour manager summed up the situation when he wrote:

No one is likely to dispute that the present labour situation is causing considerable anxiety throughout the country. After all, it is only natural after what has had to be endured during the past five years, that difficulties have cropped up and have had to be encountered. The trouble, unfortunately, is not confined to any one class or trade. It could be easily understood that in certain trades a considerable amount of dislocation had to take place, and that in consequence large numbers of men, both skilled, semi-skilled, and unskilled, have been thrown on the Labour market, and, in the case of men returning from the Army to civil life, they have often been unable to resume their original occupations. This, in itself, made it tolerably certain that labour troubles of sorts would result.

So far as the motor trade was concerned, however, there should have been no reason for trouble of this kind. And in particular, it appears to me that there is no just reason why there should be trouble with men engaged with this Company, or with the whole commercial vehicle industry for that matter. During the War Period it was generally understood that a great trade boom was to be ours in the future. This trade boom is here, and now, but we are not yet by any means 'at full stretch'.

This is almost entirely the result of the practice of restricted output. Workers certainly have just cause for anxiety owing to the considerably increased cost of living. But the question of profiteering has now been taken up by the Government, and if only all workers, whatever their rating, make increased effort, the cost of living must, in the near future, be more nearly approaching that of pre-war days, even if it never again attains it.

'We have the men, we have the plant, and we have the Orders too.' Then, why on earth, not 'get a move on'? From my own experience I know that the average British workman has nothing to learn from the American or German workman in regard to his skill. As a matter of fact, he is in every way their superior. Then why handicap ourselves and the country by restricting our output?

One of the greatest, if not the greatest fears a workman has to encounter, is the possibility of becoming unemployed, and to overcome this it is naturally the aim of the majority of men to endeavour to secure employment with large firms of standing and repute. 'Leyland Motors' has a reputation to be envied. Think of the steady growth of the British firm of 'Leyland Motors'. The number of hands employed in 1914 was 1170. At the time of the Armistice it had reached 1250, and in addition 300 women were employed. The present number of male employees is 1821. This in itself is certain proof that the Company is a live one.

A further post-war problem for the commercial vehicle industry

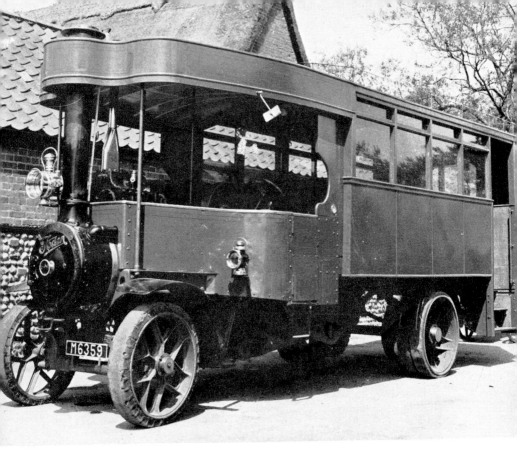

1922 Foden bus, which carried the Foden Works Band. *National Motor Museum, Beaulieu*

Hauling in the Fenland sugar beet harvest in the 1920s was this D-type Foden steam tractor of 6-tons capacity, which was built in 1922

This 6-ton wagon was delivered to J. Leonard Jnr Amusements of Manchester on 12th May 1923. It was fitted with showman's equipment,
including a belt-driven generator.

Halley, mid 1920s. *National Motor Museum, Beaulieu*

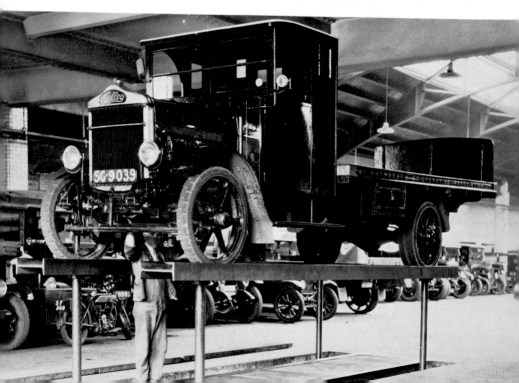

Thornycroft A1 six-wheeler, 1926. *National Motor Museum, Beaulieu*

A forerunner of the Agri-tractor, this steam tractor entered service with Bartle & Co. on 18th November 1926. It was the only one of its kind and was a special experimental model

Two Scammell
articulated lorries,
1928. *National
Motor Museum,
Beaulieu*

This special 1928
D-type Foden
steam tractor
with a 6-ton
capacity was
operated by F.
Parker & Co.
of Ancoats,
Manchester

The Sutton Ely, Cambridgeshire-based company of F. Derby & Sons, operated this Foden E-undertype six-wheeler steamer of 12 tons, probably in the late 1920s. It featured a vertical boiler with shaft drive to the double-drive bogie

This Speed 12 steam lorry was a Foden demonstration vehicle built in 1929. Seen here on trade plates it featured a 6 × 4 configuration utilizing a double-drive bogie at the rear

This 1929 6 × 4 E-undertype Foden steamer with tipper body was operated by J. G. Shields of Derby

Scammell articulated lorry, 1929. *National Motor Museum, Beaulieu*

The Morris–Commercial six-wheeler of 1929/30. Used in the Sudan by Major Court-Treatt in the production of the film *Stampede* for British Instructional Films Ltd, it crossed some 10,000 miles of country of the roughest description. *National Motor Museum, Beaulieu. (Courtesy of Major Court-Treatt)*

was the failure of members of the House of Commons to accept that the future of road transport was vital to the prosperity of the nation. In September 1919 a deputation of commercial vehicle manufacturers, which included Raymond Dennis and Henry Spurrier, saw government officials in an effort to have a temporary tariff imposed on imported foreign commercial vehicles. They were worried about the effects of foreign competition and wished to safeguard their interests at a time when American-built vehicles were making an impact in Britain. Some glimmer of hope appeared for the manufacturers when W. Joynson Hicks said in a speech at the annual C.M.U.A. lunch that '. . . there are those in the House who believe, even allowing for the power of the railways and the influence of the dock community, more and more in the future of the road as the controlling factor in the commerce, industry and trade of the country. . . .'

The cost of replacement of commercial vehicles was also causing problems. Vehicles commandeered under the War Office's subsidy scheme in 1914 were obsolete by 1919, and the replacement cost beyond the financial resources of many operators. A number of returned ex-servicemen wished to set up as hauliers but found the cost even of a second-hand vehicle to be too high with their limited funds. A 15 cwt van cost about £200, a 2-ton lorry £300, and a 3-ton lorry £500. A 5-ton steamer with rubber tyres was nearer £900. However two ex-servicemen who used their initiative to found a successful firm of commercial vehicle manufacturers were Robert and Herbert Seddon, who in 1919 began by using a Commer vehicle with chain drive, solid tyres and oil lamps in the Manchester area. Their famous company originated from this humble beginning.

In the immediate post-war years there was also a general lack of knowledge as to the future of petrol supplies, and one informed engineer claimed that the world supplies could not possibly last more than three years.

In reality there had been a considerable amount of muddled thinking on the subject of petrol supplies ever since the beginning of the century. A consensus of opinion showed that the majority of those in the motor industry thought that the United States of America would need every gallon of her own petrol supplies and in consequence could not be relied upon to export petrol to Britain. In 1906 the Motor Union had offered a prize for the best essay on 'The Manufacture and Introduction of Cheap Alcohol as a Motor Fuel' and the Royal Agricultural Society put forward a suggestion that a suction gas plant capable of being fitted to the frame of a vehicle would solve the petrol problem. Between 1905 and 1912 various unsuccessful experiments were made with paraffin vaporizers, and in

1909 two Hastings engineers produced a vehicle which ran on coal gas. During the war many firms ran their vehicles on coal gas and in 1917 a special gas demonstration was held at Thornycrofts' service depot at Pimlico.

The price of petrol had fluctuated during these years. In 1906 it was 1s. 4d. per gallon. Six years later it had been reduced to 1s. 2½d. before once again increasing. One poet, with apologies to Shelley, wrote:

> Hail to thee, blythe spirit!
> Oil thou never wert –
> Priced one-and-nine or near it
> Per gallon at the start
> Of war – but now thy dearness
>   breaks my sadden'd heart.
>
> Higher still and higher
> Up in price thou springest;
> Me, thy would-be buyer
> In the blues thou flingest.
> From exhaust thou pourest; thy scented
>   way thou wingest.

By August 1920 the price had risen steeply to 4s. 3½d. a gallon – but from this peak price it dropped steadily until it was 1s. 6½d. by 1923. On a lighter note is the anecdote of the motor hearse whose driver pulled up at a country garage. 'Can I fill up here?' asked the driver. The garage proprietor glowered at the hearse and replied, 'Depends what with. Do you want my spirit or my body?'!

5

In February 1919 an article had appeared in the *Daily News* written by Sidney Webb and entitled 'Transport is King'. He began the article:

There is something very English in the introduction, under the Ten Minutes Rule, practically without notice, and as if it were a mere trifle, of the Bill establishing a Ministry of Ways and Communications. This Ministry, if all goes well, means the beginning of a revolution in our whole transport system; and upon transport our commercial prosperity and social life nowadays depend. Five hundred years ago we were still living in a 'town economy'. Each town, almost each village, existed substantially by and unto itself. Now there is not a hamlet in the land which is not involved by a thousand ties of economic and social interest with all the rest of the nation. Not cotton or coal, but transport is king.

Hitherto we have left the great business of transport (with the one exception of municipal enterprise in tramways) to private enterprise. We have relied upon the stimulus of private profit to provide the nation with its channels of circulation. These have accordingly grown up haphazard. There has been neither the co-ordination which alone can create efficiency, nor as we now find, the competition which may secure cheapness. The Home Secretary, who is the child of the age, told the House of Commons on Wednesday night with an assured complacency that it was 'not altogether to the public good that private interest should be the main stimulus'. We are passing into the domain of public services. What the Government proposes is nothing less than the systematic organization of the whole transport service of the community. . . .

Sidney Webb was not the only opponent of the formation of the new Ministry, for it was evident that opposition was mounting amongst those directly interested in mechanical road transport. The Royal Automobile Club, for example, was convinced that the control of the roads should remain distinct from that of other means of communication, whilst other bodies considered that the Road Board, disbanded on the creation of the Ministry of Transport, should be reconstituted under the chairmanship of a Cabinet Minister. One of the chief fears of the opponents of the Ministry was that if control of the roads was placed in the hands of a Minister dominated by railway influence, then road traffic would not receive impartial fair treatment. Experience in other parts of the world had proved that when rail and road management was vested in the same hands, there was a tendency to starve road transport in order that it did not compete with railways. Consequently, the idea was put forward that if the Government either owned or controlled the railways of Britain then pressure would be applied to ensure that an adequate return upon the capital invested in the railways was available, even if such return prevented money being spent upon new roads and benefits to road transport. Road ideologists explained that more than

HIGHWAY ROBBERY!

£30 000000 was needed to restore British roads to their pre-war condition, and that in addition many important roads were inadequate to support commercial traffic whilst many bridges were too weak to support lorries laden up to their legal limit.

Despite such farsighted fears, the new Ministry of Transport was created in the summer of 1919 under the chairmanship of Sir Eric Geddes. One consequence of the establishment of the Ministry was the disbanding of the Road Board.

Geddes, born in 1875 at Agra where his father was a civil engineer, worked as a young man in the United States, being employed as a brakesman on the Baltimore and Ohio railroad, as a lumberjack and as a labourer in a steel works. Eventually he returned to India where he managed a forestry estate which involved the administration of fifty miles of light railway. He decided to leave India in 1906 when he was offered a job with the North Eastern Railway. His ability was soon recognized by his directors, and at the outbreak of the First World War he was deputy general manager. By 1916 he had won the confidence of Lloyd George, who appointed him director general of transportation on the staff of the commander-in-chief of the British Army in France. Later he became inspector general of transportation for all theatres of war with the honorary rank of major-general. Subsequently he was appointed controller of the Navy with the temporary and honorary rank of vice-admiral. In July 1916 he became unionist Member of Parliament for the borough of Cambridge and two months later First Lord of the Admiralty and a member of the Privy Council. Lloyd George appointed him to his Imperial War Cabinet and invited him to become first Minister of Transport. His appointment was greeted with delight by those who hoped to ensure a railway monopoly but with reservations by those who wished to see the future growth of road transport encouraged.

On 7th July *The Times* published a leading article on the subject under the heading 'Parliament and the Transport Bill'.

When the House of Commons today resumes consideration of the Report stage of the Transport Bill we trust some attention will be paid to the apparently unusual procedure of Sir Eric Geddes, who at present technically occupies the position of Minister without portfolio. In the official Parliamentary reports he is termed Minister-designate of Ways and Communications. The expression hardly seems permissible, since no one has any right to assume that the Bill will be passed by Parliament in its present form. Sir Eric Geddes appears to be disregarding the authority of Parliament with the bland connivance of the Government, who are far too often guilty of the same unconstitutional offence. Lord Robert Cecil remarked on Friday that he was surprised by the extent to which 'war mind' still prevails in Government circles. We strongly hope that the spirit

93

of determination and unity which led the nation to victory in the war may long continue; but if Lord Robert Cecil was thinking of the tendency to resort to extra-constitutional methods which remains prevalent among Ministers and their satellites, we entirely agree with him. Whatever else happens it is imperative that we should get the administration of the country back to constitutional lines as quickly as possible. Sir Eric Geddes is a conspicuous example of the continued perversity of the 'war mind'. He seems to be proceeding on the calm assumption that the Transport Bill will be forced through Parliament, and in some respects is acting as though it is already law. He has gathered around him a staff of war knights and generals and colonels and other officers, principally drawn from the management of the North Eastern Railway. At his temporary offices in Whitehall he has, after the fashion of the modern Minister, collected a large staff of clerks, much as a magnet attracts steel filings. He has chosen a brigadier-general, admittedly of great capacity, to look after roads, and has assigned London traffic to another nominee. What right has Sir Eric Geddes to assume that when this Bill emerges from Parliament he will be in charge of roads at all? We sincerely trust that roads will be removed from his control. It is an insult to Parliament for a Minister to take it for granted that he will be able to beat down all opposition and to act without regard to the possible decisions of the Legislature. Before the war no Minister would have ventured on such a course. Sir Eric Geddes was justified in summoning technical assistance in framing the Bill, but nothing more. It is no answer to say that some of these railway dignitaries are being paid by their companies. So long as the taxpayer is making good a huge railway deficit, they are being paid by the country. And who is paying the staff of clerks? We hope that Parliament, whose authority is in question, will look into the matter . . .

The Times leader continued by criticizing certain clauses of the Bill and certain 'concessions' which had been made by the Government. It ended by stating:

The 'concession' in regard to roads is equally fantastic. There is to be an unpaid advisory committee of ten members, five representing highway authorities, and five representing users of road traffic. All are to be chosen by Sir Eric Geddes 'after consultation with the interests concerned' and we know by experience the kind of committee he will select. This precious body will have no executive authority. It is merely 'to make see'. The truth is that the bargain made by Mr Joynson Hicks and his associates was political, and had no relation to the merits of the Bill or the needs of the community. We wish that Mr Joynson Hicks had been courageous enough to adhere to his original resolve to press for the confinement of the Bill to railways and canals. That is the only possible remedy for this unworkable example of legislative megalomania.

By 1921 many of the scars of the war were healing. The foundation of the British Legion and the erecting of war memorials in towns and on village greens acted as a permanent reminder of the war years, but the nation was beginning to readjust itself to peacetime conditions. Income tax was reduced by a shilling in the pound, the birth-rate began to fall, and the death-rate declined due to improved medical services, improved hygiene and better housing. It was the era of Horatio Bottomley, and John Bull, of Steve Donoghue, and the Prince of Wales being captain of the Royal and Ancient. Outwardly it appeared that Britain's economy was booming, but inwardly the economy was in an unhealthy state and trade was beginning to fail. In January 1921 the general manager of Leyland, C. B. Nixon, had written in the house magazine:

Mention of a prosperous New Year, with the present trade outlook, would appear to be almost a mockery. We must, however, look for the causes of the present depression, and every one of us do what we can to remove them.

During the War, we have all had so much more work to do than we could do or wanted to do, that we have got into the habit of thinking that there is always plenty of work, and that no effort is necessary to find it.

We are now learning that for various reasons it is sometimes impossible to find work, and, I feel sure, that we must all now regret that we did not do our best when the Armistice came and that we failed to appreciate the great opportunity that we had of doing well at that time for ourselves and for the firm.

Only this week, as I write, when we are, unfortunately, on short time and have had to take steps for the further reduction of hours, a possible opportunity occurs of getting very substantial orders for a new model for delivery this coming Summer, provided a sample chassis be produced by the end of February. I hope that everyone will help to that end, and that no obstructions will be placed in the way of obtaining this important result.

As an example of the kind of help we want I may cite a case. When the Moulders' Strike was in progress here, I sent over to Belgium for castings; and a firm of pattern makers there made a complete set of cylinder patterns between four o'clock on Saturday afternoon and the following Monday evening. This is the kind of spirit we must have in this country, if we are not going to lose all our trade to other nations.

The first lesson, therefore, is that we must adapt ourselves to the business that is available and put ourselves about to the extent of strenuous effort to secure that business.

Coming now to the reason why there is so little business available. The reason is not that people do not want machines: there never were more or better enquiries, but people simply cannot buy because they have not got the money to purchase with. Some people appear to think that the country can be carried on without capital, and I can only wish that they might have experienced some of the worries and difficulties with which the Directors have had to contend during the last twelve months, due to this world shortage of capital.

Six months later he detailed further causes of the depression under the title 'The Slump':

A contract for 100 reconditioned vehicles for the Greek Government and another to overhaul several hundred lorries, the property of the Royal Flying Corps, have kept Ham Works fairly fully employed. As Ham is only a great repair shop, making no material itself, these contracts brought a considerable amount of business to Head Works at Leyland, which we should not otherwise have had. The first of these contracts has been completed, and the second is nearing completion. The amount of ordinary business going forward is not nearly sufficient to keep either works fully employed.

We have been endeavouring to obtain a large order in Russia, but it is quite possible that the whole of this business may go to Germany as, on account of the different conditions there, German manufacturers are able to quote very much lower prices than we can.

We are experiencing very severe competition from Italy and other countries, where the rate of exchange operates as a severe handicap. We have our backs to the wall. We cannot here discuss the world-wide causes which have brought about the present state of affairs; what we have to do is face the results. To get business, we have to reduce prices to a very large extent, even if there is no profit and only enough to pay interest on loans and wages on a considerably lower scale than at present. The alternative would be to shut down altogether.

Those employees who are also share-holders of the Company know that we were unable to pay a dividend on our ordinary shares last year, and that the likelihood of a dividend this year is very remote.

We are cutting our losses on the fall in prices and already have made a reduction of 10 per cent. in all chassis and body prices, but it is necessary to make far bigger reductions before we can secure this country's fair share of the foreign trade. This reduction can come about only by a reduction of wages being made, slightly in advance of the reduction in the cost of living. Those of you who follow the state of affairs in several competitive countries will know that in America in particular very substantial reductions amounting to about 25 per cent have been agreed to in all the principal branches of industry, these reductions will inevitably make competition from America keener even than it is to-day in the very near future.

Only recently, particulars of a contract awarded by the Victorian Government – one of our own colonies – for electrical apparatus to America, has come to our notice. In this case, the contract was placed with America at £379 000, representing a saving of £200 000 on the best British offer; this is just given as an example, for hundreds of cases of the same kind are occurring every week.

Despite the pessimism of many commercial vehicle manufacturers, the year 1922 saw the foundation of Scammells. During the first years of the reign of Queen Victoria, George Scammell had established a business which had gained fame as wheelwrights and specialist coach-builders of carts and vans. From this business evolved a flourishing company in Spitalfields, London, selling and maintaining steam wagons and small trucks. The practical experience gained during the years of the First World War made the company appreciate that by pulling a trailer a truck could gain considerable pay-load. From this appreciation the first Scammell articulated lorry was derived in 1919. During tests the vehicle pulled a load of almost eight tons up West Hill, Highgate, in second gear, and reached a speed of 18 m.p.h. on the level. In 1921 new premises were acquired in Tolpits Lane, Watford, and Scammells manufactured a 2000–gallon fuel-oil tanker for Mex Ltd. The records show that this was the first articulated tanker built in Britain, and was the object of much admiration at the 1921 Olympia Motor Show where Scammell's truck advertisement carried the headline 'Seven Tons at Three Ton Speed and Cost'.

The economic slump of the 1920s had crucial repercussions at Sandbach, for members of the Foden family decided to emigrate to Australia. At the end of the war William Foden's sons, Reg and J. E. (Ted), joined the family business. Both had been educated at Rossall, and Reg, two years older than Ted, had served in the Royal Flying Corps in 1918. His younger brother began his commercial career by serving his apprenticeship in the erecting shop, the garage and various other departments before graduating to the drawing office. In the garage the steam wagons were tested by the process of attaching a belt to a propeller approximately three feet in diameter, thus finally achieving the particular horse-power required for each individual vehicle. These tests were followed by road tests. The vehicles were all fitted with solid rubber tyres and had a single rear-sprung bogie and chain steering. All chain-steering vehicles suffered the disadvantage of a severe kickback if a stone was struck or a pothole encountered. It was not uncommon on these occasions for the driver to break his wrist. After two years at Sandbach J. E. (Ted) Foden went to London on the sales side of the business. Orders were not easy to acquire since many local councils and private hauliers were purchasing ex-War Department stock which had seen service in France. However, one order which caused great excitement at Sandbach was for a timber-carrying vehicle for the Sandringham estate. Ted Foden had to go to Buckingham Palace to receive the order. Understandably wishing to celebrate once he had been given the order, he went to the Ritz Hotel. Being abstemious, he ordered an orange juice – the inflated price of which dampened his pleasure when he was brought the bill, and he realized that prices in Sandbach and the West End of London varied considerably! The Sandringham timber lorry was fitted with a hooter which sounded

'Toot-toot'. Years later the Duke of Windsor told Ted Foden that he remembered as a boy how much he had enjoyed blowing the hooter!

By 1924 trade was depressed and orders from customers almost unobtainable. One weekend Ted Foden returned to Sandbach to be greeted by his fifty-five-year-old father remarking, 'Ted, we are all going to Australia in a fortnight's time.' 'All' included William Foden, his wife, sons Ted and Reg and Reg's wife Nancy and her father Louis Fitton. The family sailed on the P&O ship S.S. *Mootan*, arriving in Melbourne in January 1925. A large house was rented, and eventually nineteen packing cases, each weighing two tons, arrived from England with the family furniture. Mrs William Foden was a keen collector of *objet d'art*, and the contents of the packing cases contained Louis XVI tables, Sheraton secretaires, and a pair of urns which had been given by Queen Victoria to the Czar and Czarina of Russia, smuggled to Wales after the Russian Revolution and sold to her.

Also shipped from Sandbach was William Foden's 1921 Silver Ghost Rolls-Royce and Ted Foden's three-litre Bentley. Such magnificent machines caused quite a stir in Melbourne Society! After looking at many properties William Foden decided to buy Minembah, a 8760-acre station fifty miles north of Newcastle in New South Wales. It seemed that the entire family were happily established in their new existence amidst the comparative solitude of the Outback. The first dissenter was Ted Foden, who decided after two years surrounded by sheep and cattle that he longed to return to England. After discussions with his father he sailed home, stopping off in Ceylon for a month where amongst other incidents he narrowly missed an encounter with a rogue elephant!

On his return he went to Sandbach and asked his uncle Edwin Richard Foden (also known as Ted) for a job. To his surprise his uncle referred him to the general manager Major Kyffin with the comment, 'I'm not the boss any more, you'd better ask Kyffin'. The reasons for such a comment illustrated the position of Fodens at the time. Before his death in 1911 the founder, Edwin Foden, had remarried, and his second wife became a substantial shareholder in the company on his death. She was not on the best of terms with the children of her husband by his first marriage, and attempted to undermine their authority. Trade was bad, Sam Twemlow had died in 1927, and a succession of general managers lacking in ability did not advance the prestige of Fodens in the opinion of potential customers. Goodwill was lost, the value of the shares slumped and the quality of production went down.

Despite the difficulties of the situation Ted Foden was given a job on the sales side, with his headquarters at Bedford. His task was virtually impossible for few customers were prepared to buy a 'steamer'. To add to his difficulties a new general manager, Wood Whittle, was determined to eliminate from the firm all the remaining members of the Foden family. The position became so intolerable that Edwin Richard Foden made the decision to branch out on his own. Calling his new business E.R.F., he established a works almost opposite Fodens, using an old greenhouse as his first workshop. About a dozen technicians from the Elworth works joined him, as did his son Denis and his nephew Ted. From the outset E.R.F. concentrated on building diesel-powered vehicles, believing correctly that the day of the steamer was virtually over. Components were bought from other manufacturers and merely assembled at the E.R.F. works. In the early days of E.R.F. the bodies for the vehicles were made by the local Sandbach firm of J. H. Jennings. Ted Foden was given the job of salesman – with the dubious salary that he could keep any of the 15 per cent discount offered to customers that he could persuade them not to demand. The first sale he made was successfully completed without the customer ever being told that there might be a discount! As the vehicle was sold for £1200 Ted made a handsome profit for himself of £180.

Meanwhile the situation across the road at Fodens was deteriorating further. So bad did it become that the buyer, the chief draughtsman, the sales manager and a few others decided that there was only one solution. Mr William Foden must be persuaded to return from Australia. Unbeknown to these men, William Foden was intending to take a holiday in England, so their telegram of hopeful plea proved acceptable. When he arrived at Sandbach, William Foden was appalled at the state of affairs and immediately realized that he had no option but to salvage the fortunes of the company. He called together those who had sent him the telegram, explained that he would have to make a brief return visit to Minembah, but that if he could count on 100 per cent support from the Foden employees he would come back to Sandbach and labour unstintingly to put the firm back on its feet. Such a promise was exactly in keeping with the senior technicians' hopes for the future. A new era in the history of the company was about to dawn. . . .

The return of William Foden, a man respected by all those who came into contact with him, marked the turn of the tide for Fodens. His son Ted, realizing he could not compete against his father, resigned from E.R.F. and returned to Fodens, where the decision was taken to no longer concentrate on the building of steamers but instead to build diesel-powered vehicles. This decision, which William Foden had advocated in letters written from Australia, was tanta-

99

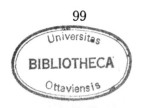

mount to leaving the manufacture of steamers entirely in the capable hands of the Sentinel Company. The first diesel Foden was built in 1931. The vehicle, fitted with a five-cylinder Gardner engine, was demonstrated to various firms, including Joseph Rank Ltd, to whom it was explained that the vehicle could work all day for about two shillings, since oil fuel was only 2¾d. a gallon and the vehicle could do fifteen miles to the gallon. It was finally sold to S. Jackson & Sons, Coal Merchants of Crewe. One of those particularly interested in diesel Fodens was Sir Malcolm Campbell, who was chairman of a company which intended to build a wall across the Wash in Lincolnshire and create a car-racing track amidst the reclaimed land. The company had bought a stone quarry with a capacity of several million tons, and were anxious to acquire a vehicle which could operate economically hauling the stone to the building site at the edge of the Wash. After demonstrations the company ordered a hundred of the new Foden vehicles. Tragically this order was cancelled when Britain went off the Gold Standard in the autumn of 1931. However, Fodens persevered, manufacturing about five of these vehicles each week, for they knew their reliability and toughness. By the mid-1930s many of them in the service of hauliers were working around the clock. One such lorry was being driven in the daytime from Liverpool to Hull loaded with flour, and during the night returning with another driver and another load. In those days there was the constant problem of fuel replacement on long journeys. Many diesel vehicles carried spare fuel tanks, for garages did not begin to stock and sell fuel oil until 1932.

Once Fodens decided to build only diesel-powered vehicles, the problem arose as to how to dispose of some fifty second-hand steamers. Luckily a Birmingham operator offered to buy the entire fleet! When William Foden arrived at the 1935 Olympia Motor Show shortly after his return to Sandbach he knew that his firm had only three orders for vehicles on their books. It was not a situation that he relished. During the show it became obvious that many past customers were delighted to see him back in harness and before the end of the show the orders had rolled in thick and fast. Even amongst his competitors there was a feeling of goodwill illustrated by an incident concerning a Foden and a Leyland. Shortly before the show, a Foden had broken down on the road and had been towed to a repair shop by a Leyland. A photographer, sensing the scoop of such a picture, had seized his camera and after the photo was developed sent it to Leylands. William Foden told Henry Spurrier of the unfair publicity that such a photo could produce, and Spurrier agreed to its immediate withdrawal from circulation.

In February 1936 William Foden attended a dinner at the Elworth works given by Sir Edwin Stockton, the chairman, and his directors to the departmental heads and assistants. After speeches had been made, one of the oldest employees of the company presented William Foden with a silver cigarette case, suitably inscribed, to commemorate his return to the company and the esteem in which he was held by the staff.

6

In mid-February 1926 Mr Winston Churchill, Chancellor of the Exchequer, had received a deputation from motoring organizations who wished to explain to him personally their opinions and views upon the question of diverting a portion of the Road Fund to purposes other than roads. The commercial vehicle industry was represented by Edward Shrapnell Smith who pointed out to the Chancellor that the industry gave employment to more than 800 000 people, a number more than 100 000 in excess of that employed by the railways. The capital contained in the industry was more than £250,000 000, and the service provided by it included deliveries to three million homes a day and the transporting of six million passengers daily. He reminded Mr Churchill that in March 1920 a pledge had been given to the industry that none of the money raised in direct motor taxation under the scheme subsequently made part of the Finance Act of that year should be applied other than in the manner laid down in the Roads Act of the same year. He urged the Chancellor not to take money from the Road Fund whilst the necessity remained to repair more than 740 bridges in order that road transport could operate economically, and added that the Government should not allow the railway companies to prejudice the interests of the commercial vehicle industry. In his reply Mr Churchill impressed upon the deputation his conviction that he could not deal with the problem fully at that time without disclosing matters which would be dealt with in the Budget. He continued by stating his opinion that it seemed to go beyond the bounds of reason to expect the yield of the Road Fund to be spent entirely on roads, no matter how serious the financial situation of the nation, and no matter how poor the nation might be in other directions. He then made his views even clearer when he said, 'I would not in any way accept the constitutional theory that Parliament has not the right to deal broadly with the interests of the country as a whole in any given year, nor do I accept for a moment that the motor tax is a tax paid voluntarily by the motorists, that they have the right if they pay this tax to prescribe how it shall be spent. Such a claim is not made by any other class of taxpayers in the country.' He ended his statement with a typically Churchillian piece of oratory which sent the deputation away comparatively satisfied: '. . . It should regard it as a most lamentable and preposterous act of folly if we were to cripple and wound the whole development of this wonderful new means of transport which is one of the greatest features of our lifetime, and which unquestionably by its smooth and speedy inter-communication has added vastly to the unseen and internal trade of the country.' Only when they were far from the inspiring presence of Mr Churchill did it dawn upon some of the deputation that perhaps the Chancellor was unenthusiastic for the future of the motor industry. A month later the railway companies put before the Minister of Transport their case against road transport with the intention of securing a transference to the road hauliers of the charges which, under present legislation, fell upon the highway rates. The railway companies hoped that in future the expense of road maintenance and construction should be met from the Road Fund. Their views highlighted the bitter struggle between the railway companies and the road transport organizations which was not to be resolved for another decade.

When Mr Churchill introduced his Budget on 25th April he made clear his determination to build a part of the Budget on the diversion of some of the reserves and annual income of the Road Fund to general national purposes and to raise the scale of road taxation in respect of public service and commercial vehicles. His view was that the money raised on account of wear and tear of the roads should go to the roads, and the balance – representing the luxury and pleasure aspect – should go to the State. He took £7 000 000 from the existing Road Fund and one third of the tax yield as the proportion attributable to luxury motoring. In the House of Commons the Labour Party strenuously opposed the 'stealing of £7 000 000 from the Road Fund' on the grounds that the proposal would lessen development work which had been undertaken or contemplated, and criticized the increases in the commercial vehicle tax. However, the Budget, which did not include a tax on petrol which Churchill had considered as a possible source of additional revenue, was over-shadowed by the imminent miners' strike. On 1st May the *Daily Chronicle* stated:

Complete collapse of the Coal negotiations shortly before midnight brings the country face to face this morning with one of the gravest industrial crises in its history. The Government's subsidy to the industry ended at midnight. The owners' notices to end the old terms expired at the same time. As the miners have declined to consider working on the revised terms offered in the various districts the whole coalfield will be rendered idle. In many districts the men left work and removed their gear as their shifts ended yesterday. What help will the miners get from the rest of the labour movement? That is the vital question, and it will be answered today.

Three days later the *Daily Telegraph* announced:

The General Strike begins today. When it will end no man can say, but how it will end there can be no manner of doubt. It will fail because the Government and the people are resolute that it shall not succeed. They will repel it as a blow aimed at the very vitals of the State and at the very existence of Constitutional Government and of public freedom. Moreover there is yet another reason why it must not only fail but fail soon. That is that the vast majority of those who will come out in obedience to the summons of their Unions have no heart in the struggle.

A week later the *Daily Express* reported that

A great crowd gathered at Marble Arch yesterday afternoon to witness the arrival of a food convoy from the docks. A stream of 104 lorries, more than two miles long, passed through the gates to Hyde Park. Two or three soldiers in full service dress with steel helmets and carrying rifles were mounted on each vehicle and there were eleven armoured cars carrying machine guns in the procession. Earlier in the day two battalions of the Guards had been sent to take over the Docks . . . all was quiet in Regent's Park which had been converted into a parking ground for vehicles. A field hospital had been erected in the grounds as well as a complete machine shop and sleeping quarters for the volunteer drivers. . . .

Within a week the General Strike was over, although the coal strike continued for a further six months. There was no doubt that during the Strike, with the railways out of action, the nation was saved to a large extent by the ability of road transport to continue operating.

One commercial vehicle firm not seriously affected by the strike was Guy Motors, whose chairman, Sydney Guy, stated: 'During the General Strike we found to our surprise that only a very few did not work.' Sydney Guy, who had gained his practical engineering experience with the Belliss and Morcom Steam Engineering Company, later joined the Sunbeam Motor Company of Wolverhampton, where he became works manager. At the end of 1913 he resigned from Sunbeam, and in May 1914 his company, Guy Motors Ltd, was

Morris-Commercial six-wheeler, 1930. *National Motor Museum, Beaulieu*

With a 10-ton payload capacity and a 6 × 4 configuration utilizing a double-drive bogie manufactured by Fodens, this vehicle was fitted with 6LW Gardner engine

A.E.C. Mammoth Major, 1932. *National Motor Museum, Beaulieu*

An early Foden oiler with 'brown loaf' van body by Beadle, *circa* 1933. *National Motor Museum, Beaulieu*

A.E.C. plus draw-bar trailer, 1933. *National Motor Museum, Beaulieu*

When this Foden vehicle appeared in 1934 its design was heralded as years
ahead of its time. It was designated the DG4 model

Armstrong Saurer six-wheeler, 1934. These trays were filled with bricks while the lorry might be elsewhere on another job, and loaded onto the vehicle by the derrick attached to the lorry. Time was thereby saved and handling costs reduced. *National Motor Museum, Beaulieu*

Built in 1935 and powered by a 3-cylinder Gardner diesel engine, this Foden 2-ton truck featured a cab constructed of a wood frame with metal cladding

Ford V8 six-wheeler conversion, 1936. *National Motor Museum, Beaulieu*

William Foden (1869–1964)

The year 1938 saw the Foden Motor Works' Band the proud holders of the Crystal Palace Trophy. Pictured here outside Middlewich Manor are the members of the band with Mr Willie Foden *(seated left of the trophy)*

Bedford ambulance. *National Motor Museum, Beaulieu*

Centaur tank manufactured at the Foden works during the Second World
War

One of the six prototype 17-lb anti-tank gun towers which were manufactured for the British Army during the Second World War

One of 1750 army trucks supplied by Fodens to the British Army during the Second World War

Scammell 4 × 4 tractor in action at West Watford sub electricity station 1952. *National Motor Museum, Beaulieu*

floated, and commenced manufacture at Fallings Park, Wolverhampton. One of Sydney Guy's original ideas was to build commercial vehicles with a much lighter form of pressed steel frame than the accepted extremely reliable but inordinately heavy frame used on the majority of commercial vehicles. Guy Motors were hardly established when the First World War shattered the peace of Europe. The Ministry of Munitions took over many of Guy's vehicles and supplied them to Russia, whilst the factory became the largest manufacturers of firing mechanisms for depth-charges in the country. The war over, Guys returned to the building of lorries, buses and private motor cars. Some of the cars incorporated the first automatic chassis lubrication system which brought the caustic comment from an agent: 'I see that you have a telephone in every bedroom.' In 1920 Guy Motors produced its first special vehicle for cross-country work, known as 'the farmers special'. By 1924 Guy Motors published an advertisement showing a feather in the radiator cap for each important repeat order received from customers. Eventually so many feathers had to be incorporated that a new symbol was evolved – of a Red Indian chief – which became the figurehead on all Guy motors. In the same year supplies of special trucks were made to the Admiralty, War Office and Crown Agents to the Colonies. These vehicles had caterpillar tracks replacing rear wheels. The company had always prided itself on its relationship with its employees, and therefore the lack of absenteeism during the General Strike was not cause for comment. However, when the strike was ended, the management made it clear that although they were not interested as to whether or not their work people were members of a trade union, they considered that it was in the company's interest that the fact should be disclosed. Consequently the company formed a works committee which had proportional representation, and issued a declaration form which had to be signed by all Guy employees:

Are you a member of a Trade Union?
What Union (if any)?
   I agree, if engaged, to observe all the rules and regulations of Guy Motors Ltd, and particularly those special rules relating to the avoidance of disputes as follows:
   I agree not, under any circumstances, to cease work or go slow until the matter under dispute has been reported in writing within 48 hours' notice by the Works Committee to the General Works Manager who the firm undertake will reply within 48 hours. Failing a satisfactory reply the matter, in writing, shall be referred to the Managing Director with 48 hours' notice, who undertakes to reply within 48 hours. If the reply is unsatisfactory, the Committee can refer the matter to the Executive of the Trades Union, who will communicate with the Managing Director, and,

providing the answer received is not satisfactory, then and not until then, will I down tools.

By 1926 the economy of fitting pneumatic tyres to commercial vehicles instead of using solid tyres was becoming apparent. Admittedly the initial cost of pneumatic tyres was higher but the advantages outweighed this cost. Figures published to prove these advantages stated that although the pneumatics cost 38 per cent more than solids, they effected a saving of 16 per cent on petrol, 12 per cent on repairs and gave an average increase in the life of the vehicle of 24 per cent. In addition vehicles fitted with pneumatic tyres had the further advantage of being able to maintain higher road speeds.

One of the problems of the 1920s was clearly stated by Sir John Thornycroft when he wrote in an article for *The Commercial Motor*:

One cannot but be a little disappointed at the way in which our foreign rivals have beaten the Old Country in the matter of production. It is very doubtful if America would have been able to get such a strong position if we had not been held back by the War. The grouping of firms with a view to making reduced numbers of types may have helped, but there, as well as here, many who have tried their hands at building vehicles have gone out of business.

We are suffering, at the present time, by not knowing to what extent legislation is likely to affect design, and it is a thousand pities that, when a Government inquiry results in certain recommendations, manufacturers are not promptly informed if those recommendations are to be adopted or not.

The British manufacturers want their own market protected, not only for their own benefit, but for that of the country generally. It is necessary that they do a large export business. Legislation which tends to produce types in this country which are not generally acceptable in our Colonies and abroad is obviously wrong. It is the fashion to-day to praise the British car with its small engine, which has resulted from the method of taxation, but anyone who has been in our Colonies and abroad knows perfectly well that we have lost many of the best markets in the world to the Americans, because they were building cars with engines which were not nearly so highly rated.

British makers of commercial vehicles cannot afford to establish their own branches all over the world and, if they try to find a good agent abroad, the chances are they will find the best for the particular place or country is primarily interested in American production and is loth to represent a British vehicle.

Thornycrofts, typical of the leading commercial vehicle manufacturers of the era, were making thirteen different chassis suitable for freight and passenger carrying work, at their Basingstoke factory, and were building a range of bodies suitable for every conceivable lorry and van including brewers' lorries, end tipping wagons, vans with solid tops and open-sided lorries. When the Commercial Motor Users Association held their annual vehicle parade in March 1927 a newly designed tank wagon caused considerable interest. Built by Thompson Bros of Bilston on a 5-ton Associated Daimler chassis, it had been commissioned by Shell Mex for the conveyance of bulk supplies of motor spirit. This tanker was the forerunner of many others built for the transport of petroleum from depots to petrol stations. During the year Fodens also brought out a new 6-ton under-type wagon which was put into service with the Co-operative Whole-sale Society after extensive trials. The wagon, to some extent revolutionary in technical design, proved so successful that production on a large scale was commenced at the Sandbach factory. One of the reasons for this production was the conviction of the Foden directors that everything pointed to heavier and heavier loads being carried in the future, despite the proposed regulations of the Ministry of Transport. At the same time as the Foden engineers were successfully experimenting with their 6-ton steam wagon, other engineers were developing the diesel engine. Engineers on both sides of the English Channel were convinced by the mid-1920s that the use of diesel engines would result in economy of fuel due to high thermal efficiency and the reduction of fire risk due to the use of fuels of high flash point. Their tests proved, however, that there was much further development to be carried out before the diesel engine could rival the petrol engine for use in commercial vehicles. Not until 1929 did the first British diesel lorry – built by Kerr Stuart of Stoke – make its appearance. During the same year Scammells built the world's largest truck – a 100–ton gross heavy tractor. The tractor had a speed of 5–6 m.p.h. and consumed a gallon of petrol every mile. There was telephonic communication between the driver of the motive unit and the rear steersman who was responsible for signalling overtaking traffic and for all reversal operations. Two unusual loads carried by the tractor were the main girders for the new Cumberland Hotel at Marble Arch, and a 95-ton whale washed up on the English coast.

The development of the high-speed oil engine began with the work of Ackroyd Stewart and Dr Diesel towards the end of the nineteenth century. To Stewart is owed a debt for his practical development of a method of fuel injection. To Dr Diesel the theoretical conception and the commercial development of a rational heat engine with the characteristic ability to burn a cheap fuel. Rudolph Diesel was a remarkable man whose death in September 1913 was surrounded by mystery. On the night of Monday, 29th September, he left Ghent to attend the Annual General Meeting of the Consolidated Diesel Engine Manufacturers Ltd, in London. Accompanied by the chief engineer of Carels Frères, and by M. George Carels, who was also a director of Consolidated Diesel Engine Manufacturers, the be-spectacled and bearded Dr Diesel travelled across the Channel from Antwerp to Harwich aboard the Great Eastern Railway's steamer *Dresden*. The three men dined together and retired to their cabins at 10 p.m., having discussed a new factory at Ipswich which they were to visit the following day. In the morning as the steamer approached Harwich it was discovered that Dr Diesel's bed had not been slept in. All his personal luggage was in the cabin, his keys on the dressing table and his travelling clock placed so that it could be seen from the bed. When every other passenger had disembarked Dr Diesel's two companions and the ship's officers made a thorough search but with-out finding a trace of the eminent German mathematician. A signifi-cant factor was that Dr Diesel had received a landing ticket soon after the steamer left Antwerp. When these landing tickets handed in by disembarked passengers were checked at Harwich one was missing. The conclusion was that Dr Diesel had fallen overboard.

Fifty-six-year-old Dr Diesel, who had been born in Paris of German parents, was known to be suffering from insomnia and was not in the best of health. During the last few months of his life he had been actively engaged in experiments with a new type of Mexican oil which he hoped would prove cheaper than any other. He did not make frequent trips to England, but in November 1912 he had come to London before travelling to the Clyde to attend trials aboard S.S. *Fordenau*, which was fitted with diesel engines. The Consolidated Diesel Engine Manufacturers were financially involved in the Mexican oil experiments, and the chairman's announcement of Dr Diesel's disappearance caused confusion and alarm amongst share-holders at the A.G.M. The meeting was adjourned for a month whilst further investigations were made. The following day rumours spread that Dr. Diesel had not crossed on the *Dresden*, although he had boarded the ship with M. Carels. These rumours were discoun-ted by the proof that the missing man had been seen dining with his companions after the *Dresden* had left Antwerp. A large reward was offered for any information, but none was forthcoming until a fort-night later fishermen laying their nets at the mouth of the Scheldt discovered the body of a man in an advanced state of decomposition. From various items including an eyeglass and a diary it was assumed to be the body of the doctor. A month later a meeting of Dr Diesel's creditors was held in Munich. It had become evident since his dis-appearance that his financial affairs were in a calamitous state, and also that he was fully aware of the situation. Shortly before his death he had realized all his assets including surrendering life policies. At the time of his disappearance he left debts and mortgages amounting to more than £50000. His family were completely unaware of the true state of his affairs, being under the impression that he was a rich man.

A tribute to the British commercial vehicle industry was given in September 1928 by Henry Ford when he created his museum at Dearborn. Remembering a steam wagon that he had admired on a visit to Manchester in 1920, he insisted on acquiring a similar steamer to illustrate the highest development of steam transport on British roads. The steamer eventually acquired was a Foden, and Ford's representative was able to explain: 'We have procured a Foden steam wagon and this is a typical specimen of the type that Mr Henry Ford saw running around the English cities. It is in reasonably good mechanical condition, and the appearance of the condition of the paintwork and bodywork is quite nice, as it has been very well kept.' The steam wagon was shipped to Henry Ford's museum aboard the S.S. *Baltic*.

In October 1929 the C.M.U.A. held its twenty-fifth anniversary banquet at the Savoy Hotel. The gathering was graced by the presence of H.R.H. the Prince of Wales, who proposed the toast 'The Association'. In the course of his speech the Prince emphasized his belief that the problem of road congestion was very serious and suggested that it would deteriorate still further if commercial vehicle users and the owners of private cars did not get together in an effort to prevent a great battle of the roads. The Prince continued: 'With all deference to our railway companies I would say that well-maintained fleets of commercial vehicles enable our manufacturers to transport their goods to the distributors with the minimum of handling, and the small retailer has the advantage of having goods delivered right to his shop.' Other speakers at the lunch included the Minister of Transport, Mr Herbert Morrison, and the Japanese Ambassador.

Within a year of the Prince's speech Mr L. H. Pomeroy, managing director of Daimler Ltd, had made it clear that in his opinion there were only two ways to avoid traffic congestion. Firstly by the building of wide roads, and secondly by building commercial vehicles capable of maintaining high speeds. Laurence Henry Pomeroy, one of the most influential engineers in the motor industry, had been born in 1883. His father was a fanatical Radical, whose reputed ambition was the downfall of Horatio Bottomley, the member for South Hackney. Pomeroy, after being apprenticed at the North London Locomotive Works at Bow, won a Whitworth Exhibition. In 1904 he joined Humphrey & Co. and before the end of the year had designed and built a stationary gas engine. He then went to Thornycrofts at Basingtoke, but was sacked a few months later for spending too much time studying textbooks during working hours. In 1905 he was given a job at Vauxhall Motors as a junior draughtsman. Three years later fate intervened on his behalf when the chief designer became ill and twenty-five-year-old Pomeroy was asked to design a car for the R.A.C. 2000-mile trial. The car was a brilliant success and made Pomeroy's reputation. The year before the war he had won the Crompton Medal for his paper 'High Speed Engine Design'. In 1919, after designing the four-litre W-type Vauxhall known as the Prince Henry, which was extensively used as a military staff car, he left for the U.S.A. at the invitation of the President of the Aluminium Corporation. He returned to England in 1926 to become general manager of Associated Daimler, and to perfect his development of the fluid flywheel.

During 1920 and 1930 the Government had set up a Royal Commission on Transport which made three reports. The first merely recommended greater control of road traffic in the interests of public safety. The second proposed a licensing system for public service vehicles. These two reports formed the basis of the 1930 Road Traffic Act.

The third report, which was greeted by furious uproar, suggested that vehicles above four tons unladen weight should be discouraged from using the roads – and to this end it was advocated that they should be severely penalized by means of taxation. The uproar was so great that the Ministry of Transport appointed a committee under Sir Arthur Salter to examine the relationship of road transport with other transport interests – and also in particular its financial obligations. The Road Haulage Association considered that the membership of the Salter Commission was not sufficiently representative of their interests and complained bitterly, but to no avail. The Commission attempted to determine the extent to which the increased cost of roads during the past thirty years was attributable to the growth of road transport, and having assessed this, to propose scales of taxation which would provide an annual revenue equivalent to the annual maintenance costs. Another proposal from the Commission, which became known as The Salter Report, was that goods vehicles should be licensed by the Traffic Commissioners established by the 1930 Road Act. This proposal also met with the antagonism of the Road Haulage Association.

Until the publishing of the Salter Report the tax on a steam vehicle was £35 a year. The Salter Report proposed a prohibitive increase to £135 per annum. Many of those most closely connected with the steamer industry were convinced that the root cause of this increase was the influence of the petrol companies who still saw a steamer as a threat to their own interests. The report suggested that steamers were dangerous vehicles – and the general public, ever ready to object to the damage caused by flames from the steamer's chimney, agreed with the report. In consequence, steam wagons were virtually put off the road, for axle weights were restricted to eight tons and the excise licence cost based on unladen weight. It must be remembered that the solo speed limit was a maximum of 20 m.p.h., but these steamers could do 50 m.p.h. loaded.

When many of the Salter recommendations were incorporated into the Road and Rail Traffic Act of 1933 it sounded the death-knell for steam traction vehicles on the roads of Britain. It also resulted in the lowering of the efficiency of the road transport industry by increasing its cost, by limiting its activities and preventing its natural growth.

Eighteen months earlier Henry Spurrier of Leyland Motors had expressed his future views when he wrote in the *Commercial Motor*:

Road development in its stages of development has closely followed that of its predecessor, the railways. At first passengers were carried, then goods. Primarily short runs, then longer distances were dealt with, but trains stopped at each station. Then came excursion traffic, and gradually long-distance hauls and through runs from point to point without stops. At the present stage the rolling stock has become more elaborate, units are heavier and the road relaid to deal with increased weights travelling at increasing speed. Is it not possible by analogy to anticipate the line of development of road transport, with the fundamental difference that the special track is not required and the road is equally useful and available for all classes of vehicle traffic? Vehicles providing greater safety and comfort will be continually produced, units will become heavier as the main roads are constructed capable of carrying greater weights. Larger power units working more economically will be evolved to deal with the load. The railroad, like the tramway, will cease to be necessary, although possibly the old 'road' may be used for speed services or heavy hauls by motor. The internal combustion engine will be the motive power unit of the future. The engine that will be the most generally used will be one designed for a comparatively heavy-grade oil with high flash point, compression ignited, thus dispensing with carburetters and magnetos. The fuel which will be used need not, and probably will not, be the Diesel or gas-fuel oil about which so much is heard at the present time. It may be a fuel obtained from sources other than the petroleum wells, or it may be a crude oil chemically treated; whatever its source it will be a fuel basically cheaper to produce and less wasteful in production that the highly volatile petrol liquids. Fire risk will, of course, be greatly reduced. Transport in a general sense, is one of the chief weapons which mankind must use in his continual struggle to conquer space and time, hence its development must go on in the air, on the water and on land. The development of this last named form of transport will assuredly occur on the road and not on the rail. It is a simpler and more economical undertaking to build a road than a railway.

Henry Spurrier's remarks concerning the railways were not spoken lightly for he knew the great efforts being made by the railways to regain their lost goods and passenger traffic. He knew too of the powerful political lobbying on behalf of the railways, and was mistrustful of the words of politicians. Winston Churchill had once stated: 'The immense expansion of road transport by motor vehicle is an economic advantage of measureless consequence to the whole industrial life of the nation,' but such words and implications had not prevented him imposing a further duty of fourpence a gallon on petrol in his 1928 Budget, giving as his object the protection of the interests of both the railways and the coal industry.

During 1930 the big four railways who had been granted powers to operate road services by the 1928 Transport Act had made strenuous efforts to attract the business of those who needed goods to be carried to their destination. The Great Western Railway bought 250 vehicles in 1930 to bring the total number of their fleet to more than 1400 modern lorries. Rail-head distribution schemes introduced at Cardiff and Swansea proved so successful that the service was expanded to Exeter and Bristol from where villages within a thirty-mile radius were served. The L.N.E.R. were also increasing the size of their lorry fleet which had risen from 198 in 1923 to more than 800 in 1931. It was the fear of the commercial motor industry that the railways would achieve so strong a hold over the distribution of goods from railway stations to their destination that the private haulier would be forced into bankruptcy.

At a commercial vehicle dinner towards the end of the year Henry Spurrier, always an excellent raconteur, told the story of an old lady who with much waving of her umbrella induced a bus to stop – and asked the conductor if the bus was going to Leyland. On receiving the reply in the negative she said, 'But it has Leyland on the front.' The reply of the conductor was terse: 'Aye – so it has, Mum – and it also has a tiger on the front as well – but it doesn't follow that the bus is bound for the zoo.'

Leylands at this time extolled their characteristics in an unusual parody – for which they made suitable apologies to Lewis Carroll.

'You are old, Father Leyland,' the young van said,
'and your paint is no longer so bright;
Though built for four tons, you take seven instead,
Do you think at your age it is right?'

'In my youth,' the old Leyland replied to his son,
'I was built to withstand any strain,
So now I don't mind the extra odd ton.
Why, I do it again and again.'

'You are old,' said the van, 'as I mentioned before,
and your body's a tumbled down flat,
Yet your second-hand value's as high as of yore;
Pray, what is the reason for that?'

Said the old Leyland lorry, 'Now let me explain;
The fact which does most to preserve this
Is that, old though I am, I can always obtain
Spare parts and reliable service.'

'You're so old,' said the van, 'that you're almost antique;
One would say at your age you go through it,
For hundreds of miles you still cover each week;
Pray, how do you manage to do it?'

This time the old Leyland replied with less tact,
As his throttle with sentiment trembled:
'The work that I can do is just due to the fact
I was built – and not merely assembled.'

'You are old,' said the van, 'one would hardly suppose
That your upkeep's as little as ever,
Yet never an increase your maintenance shows;
What makes you so awfully clever?'

'I have answered three questions and that is enough,'
Said the old 'un, 'don't give yourself airs.
Do you think I can listen all day to such stuff?
Be off, or you'll need some repairs.'

The summer of 1931 found Britain in the midst of a financial
crisis. The Prime Minister resigned, and a National Government was
formed under Mr Ramsay MacDonald, with Mr Stanley Baldwin
and Sir Herbert Samuel in the Cabinet. In his Election Manifesto
Ramsay MacDonald announced that the present National Government had been formed to meet a swiftly approaching crisis. It
stopped borrowing, imposed economy and balanced the budget.
World conditions and internal financial weakness, however, made it
impossible for the Government to achieve its immediate object.
Sterling came off gold and the country went through a period of
recovery and readjustment during which steps of the utmost importance, nationally and internationally, were taken to secure stability
to avoid a recurrence of the recent troubles. In September, on the
resignation of Mr Herbert Morrison, Mr Percy Pybus, the Liberal
member for Harlow, was appointed as the new Minister of Transport.

Two months earlier fifty-one-year-old Mr Pybus, a director of the
English Electric Co., had become chairman of the Phoenix Assurance
Co., which had large interests in the U.S.A. He had set off on an
American tour, and it was whilst in America that he had received

an urgent wireless message from Ramsay MacDonald asking him to join the Government. He rushed to New York and caught the Cunarder *Mauretania* with only hours to spare before she sailed.

Shortly after his appointment he made it abundantly clear that he considered that the economy which might result from the use of commercial vehicles and trailers of extreme size and weight, travelling often at considerable speed, had to be related to the proper use and enjoyment of the highway by other forms of traffic, and by the general public. It also had to be related to the heavy cost of the construction and maintenance of highways and bridges to the standard necessary to carry such vehicles. His views filled many owners of commercial vehicles with misgivings as to the future. However, within six months of his appointment he had arranged for a committee to be set up to investigate the facts relating to the total costs of the highway system, including the regulation of traffic and the equitable conditions necessary for road hauliers and railways to carry on their trade. Their investigations were tardy, and received the cynical comment that 'if Moses had been a committee, the Israelites would still be in Egypt'.

In April 1932 an article by C. T. Brunner appeared in *The Times* under the heading 'Organization of Road Haulage':

Attention has lately been focused upon the road haulage industry on account of the prominence given to road competition as a cause of lower earnings by railways. Actually, the importance of this competition is often exaggerated. The net ton-miles of freight traffic for railways amount to some 17 825 704 700 a year, against an estimated total for all motor-vehicles of 4 826 611 200. When it is remembered that not more than 70 000 of the 360 000 goods vehicles registered are owned by haulage contractors, and that a great deal of collection and delivery work performed by motor-vehicles is not competitive with the railways at all, it becomes clear that the field in which competition can have had serious consequences must be very restricted.

The fact that most haulage contractors have, like the railways, suffered from reduced earnings would suggest that the whole transport industry has been hit by trade depression, and perhaps also by the increasing tendency for private firms to operate their own motor-vehicles. It is the growing popularity of privately-owned transport, and not any expansion in the haulage industry, which accounts for the steady annual growth in the total number of goods motor-vehicles registered. In making comparisons with the railways, it should be borne in mind that there are more than four times as many railway trucks in use as there are lorries, and that the average capacity of a truck is much more than four times that of a lorry.

GOODS TRAFFIC

In Germany an emergency decree last December severely restricted the operations of road hauliers, who now have to obtain special licences to operate more than 30 miles from their base. Such licences are only granted where the operator can establish a strong claim. The object is to protect the State-owned railways from competition. In Great Britain, however, the reduction in railway receipts, although serious, has been much less than in Germany, and nothing so drastic as the German licensing system is likely to be introduced. Nevertheless, it would be unwise for road operators to assume that the Government will adopt a policy of *laissez faire*. Regulation of the industry by the Area Traffic Commissioners was recommended in the Final Report of the Royal Commission on Transport and is known to be favoured by a section of the industry. Should this be introduced there can be little doubt that the railways would take a financial interest in goods transport by road, in the same way that they have done in the omnibus industry. At present they are only interested in a very small number of goods haulage businesses, and are hardly likely to extend their commitments until they have some guarantee that their investments will not be rendered worthless through new competition springing up.

The road-haulage industry has reacted to the trade depression and resulting fierce competition in rates by an extension of regular services running to a time-table at the expense of free-lance hauliers taking a load as and when they can get one. This development is a result of present industrial conditions, but it has been intensified by the Road Traffic Act, which limited hours of work to a maximum of 11 in any one day. The fixing of more reasonable speed-limits for goods vehicles is also conducive to working more exactly to a time-table. The regular service is most effective for dealing with small quantities of goods dispatched by different people to the same destination . . .

Perhaps the most interesting development in the industry in the past few months has been the formation of the Long Distance Road Haulage Association, a direct descendent of the Long Distance Road Haulage Committee of Enquiry, the body which gave rather startling evidence before the Royal Commission on Transport in favour of the licensing of hauliers and clearing-houses and their control by the Area Traffic Commissioners. The objects of the Long Distance Road Haulage Association are primarily to organize the haulage industry and provide it with a representative body which can undertake propaganda and look after the interests of the industry generally. In addition to hauliers, clearing-houses may be included in the movement. The organization of the association is on a regional basis, and, although at present it has confined its activities to its original purposes, it is undoubtedly a fact that the linking up of the industry thus brought about is proving an important consolidating force and will sooner or later produce closer working between the firms concerned than has been possible in the past.

So far, no large holding company has appeared in the haulage industry to perform the work of rationalization which the Tilling group has undertaken for the omnibus industry, and it seems probable that this process will come about in a somewhat different way, and will start from the foundation now being built up by the Long Distance Road Haulage Association. The haulage industry of the future will consist to a much less extent than to-day of small units, and develop a regional organization based on large clearing-houses controlling the running of regular services between all important centres.

In the same month a Bill was introduced into Parliament to amend the Road Traffic Act of 1930. Introducing a second reading of the Bill in the House of Lords, Lord Buckmaster began by stating that although great inventive skill had produced the internal combustion engine, no one would deny that wherever motor vehicles had gone they had completely destroyed all beauty and peace of life . . . Referring to the last part of the Bill (which provided that no goods vehicle exceeding five tons in total weight should exceed the speed of five miles an hour in any city, town or village) Lord Buckmaster said that heavy motor vans had turned the roads into railways and were in many cases nothing but liberated railway trains. Railways had to enclose their lines, but these heavy motor lorries were subject to none of the restrictions to which the railways were liable. He would rather cross blindfold the railway level crossings he knew than walk with his eyes open across some of the roads as he knew them in the country today. He had never thought that the chariot of progress was a triumphal car that scattered blessings along its track. He had always known that it was a juggernaut grinding men and nations alike beneath its wheels. . . .

Such comments made many of those who guided the destiny of the commercial vehicle industry shudder as they anticipated the consequences of such confused thought.

During the next two years Herr Hitler became German Chancellor, John Galsworthy died, Gordon Richards rode more winners than Fred Archer, and Jack Hobbs retired.

At the end of 1934 the views of some notable personalities in the commercial motor industry were published in the *Commercial Motor*. Lord Nuffield wrote:

The success of the commercial vehicle industry is really a triumph for British engineering. The vehicles that are being turned out to-day from our factories are the outcome of a great deal of close study, scientific investigation, technical achievement, and commercial initiative.

Apart from the fact that competition keeps us all on our toes, the transport industry can rely with confidence on our commercial-vehicle-producing factories to leave no stone unturned in their efforts to give still better value, not only in the vehicles themselves, in which continuity of stabilized design is very important, but also in respect of the provision of a series of services that embraces all angles of the transport operator's undertaking, and thus assist him in every way.

Mr C. W. Reeve, chairman and managing director of A.E.C., stated:

More Co-Ordination!

Railway Magnate to Railway Employee: "It's up to you now."

At present, road transport is labouring under what I have heard described as a 'welter of legislation', and when one realizes that the restrictions since 1930 alone are included in no less than three principal Acts of Parliament, and some 70 odd Orders comprising nearly 460 individual regulations as to the length, height and width of motor vehicles, their weight and speed, the roads upon which they are used, the total number which may be employed in any service, etc., this can scarcely be an incorrect statement. No one hopes more sincerely than I that wise laws will prevail, and that the road-transport industry, both for operators and manufacturers, will be freed from further irrational and restrictive measures. I think this will be so.

There will, doubtless, be much advance in the important matter of weight reduction in chassis, whilst maintaining ample strength for the conveyance of maximum pay-loads.

The increasing use of light-weight lorries, placed in service chiefly to evade the heavy taxation, is, in my opinion, not sound development of road transport. Where large quantities of material have to be transported at one time, this will lead not only to a multiplicity of running costs, but the very serious matter of congestion on the road will be aggravated. Heavy-duty vehicles would transport large loads more cheaply and efficiently.

I predict that there will be, in the not-far-distant future, greater advance in the development of the compression-ignition engine, and that this type of prime mover will enjoy a much wider application than it does at present. The most useful experimental work at present being carried out by British and foreign railways will lead to its further employment in this sphere.

There are healthy signs of a greater demand in the future, from Empire and other overseas countries, for British road-transport units. This, I think, will be the British motor vehicle manufacturers' just reward for the care and thought that they have applied to the development of their products. So far as A.E.C. vehicles are concerned, prospects from certain overseas markets are distinctly encouraging.

In March 1935 Sir Malcom Campbell set up a new world land-speed record when his Bluebird car attained speeds of 276 m.p.h. over the Daytona Beach mile. Two months later he was a guest at the annual lunch of the Road Haulage Association. When invited to make a speech he commented that he believed, sad though it might be, that the same policy towards British roads existed as had prevailed in the eighteenth century. The marvellous strides made in road transport vehicles demanded the best possible roads – but they did not exist. He added that in his opinion independently sprung wheels all round would soon be used on all classes of road vehicles to reduce the effects of road shocks. A few moments earlier the luncheon guests had received a speech from Lieutenant-Colonel J. T. C. Moore-Brabazon who, although a Member of Parliament, made a blistering attack upon his fellow members. He claimed that 'whenever the word "motor car" was mentioned they became a collection of blithering old women. The Government had dealt to road transport the most punishing body blows possible. One would think that every Member of the House of Lords travelled in a sedan chair. Soon the Government would build new roads and allow only pedestrians and cyclists to use them. . . .'

Before the end of the year Sir Herbert Austin had written an article in the *Commercial Motor* in which he insisted that trade, commerce and national prosperity depended upon efficient transport. He expressed his views succinctly when he wrote:

It is difficult to realize that only thirty years ago there was scarcely a commercial vehicle to be seen on the streets or the roads of this or any other country. That so short a time has brought about the development of a transport system which, by the way, is almost entirely reliant upon the internal combustion engine, speaks for its utility and demand, and indicates that if an industry can grow to such proportions in three decades the immensity of its future is almost beyond our powers of imagination.

Just over thirty years ago, in 1904, the total number of commercial vehicles in use in this country was about 4000. The corresponding figure for today is well over 400000, and is rising at the rate of over 20000 vehicles per year, whilst British factories are producing at the present time some 85000 vehicles per annum.

. . . There is no doubt that the tendency towards decentralization in modern town planning calls more and more for the freedom of expansion which the mobility of road transport affords, and less for the territorial limitations that the permanent way imposes. . . . Factories can now be erected outside the boundaries of the highly rated towns, and although they may be quite isolated from the railway systems they can safely rely upon the road vehicle for their supplies and the transport of their workers. I feel that this decentralization of industry will ultimately solve the unemployment problem, but its consummation depends more than anything else upon the inter-communication provided by the commercial vehicle. Hand in hand with the rise of the business motor must go the development of the roads. The old Roman axiom that a country relies upon its roads was never truer than it is today . . . to say that the future of road transport is 'in the lap of the gods' would be an understatement for actually it occupies a much more precarious position – it is in the lap of Governments, and its development depends very largely upon two factors under the control of our legislators – one arresting the mass of restrictive legislation with which the industry is at present hemmed in, and two, the carrying out of a road programme that will enable road transport to take its rightful place in the economic life of the community which its efficiency and economy warrant . . . the creation of roads to carry the growing volume of traffic in safety is one of our most urgent national problems and this factor above all others will decide the future of the commercial vehicle industry.

The future of the roads was a permanent problem. Rees Jeffreys, the chairman of the Roads Improvement Association, was constantly bringing the issue into the open. On every possible occasion he made the point that the demand for motor vehicles must finally be limited by the capacity of the public highways to support them. His fear was that the manufacturers would over-produce, and that in consequence the roads would become saturated with traffic, speeds would be reduced to a farcical level, and delays would cause havoc with delivery services. He warned the commercial vehicle industry that its interests would always be subjugated to those of the railway companies unless the industry took the trouble to defend itself. He denounced highway authorities who he claimed had failed to provide adequate roads, and were attempting to adapt modern motor traffic to inadequate roads rather than adapting the roads to the traffic. He also pointed out the iniquitous manner in which the motorist was being heavily taxed, and the equally iniquitous restrictions placed upon him. By the mid-1930s almost £75 000 000 per year was being paid by motor users in taxation, of which the Exchequer was taking some £50 000 000, and of the balance less than £5 000 000 was being spent on new roads.

The major issue not highlighted by Jeffreys was the determined policy of the railway companies to achieve a monopoly, and to deprive the road hauliers of business. Since the Road Traffic Acts of 1930 and 1933, which had bewildered many operators, virtually every application by road hauliers for an A or B carrier's licence was opposed by the railway companies who were prepared to spend thousands of pounds on legal costs to win their cases. There was little doubt that one of the reasons for their success was the lack of solidarity of the various commercial interests, and those within the commercial vehicle industry with the most foresight were convinced that it was essential to pool their resources. However, although some of those in the commercial vehicle industry thought that they were being martyred – they received comfort from the sales director of Vauxhall who claimed 'The cause of the martyr always triumphs'.

Typical of the railways' attitude was their policy towards those who wished to transport racehorses by road. The first petrol-driven horse-box had been designed by Vincents of Reading, and fitted above a 3-ton Dennis chassis. Shown at the Royal Agricultural Show at Durdham Downs near Bristol it had attracted a great deal of attention. Vincents had taken as their slogan words written by Racine: 'Who wishes to travel far – let him spare his steed', and their horse-box proved an immediate success, although it was not until the end of the First World War that they were able to build boxes in any quantity. By the mid-1920s other companies, including the Lambourn Racehorse Transport Co, founded by Sir Hugh Nugent, and

Refuse collecting vehicle manufactured in the early 1950s fitted with a S.18 crew cab and Eagle Engineering refuse collecting equipment

A Karrier Yorkshire gully emptier, *circa* 1955, supplied by Rootes Group distributors in Helsinki. The Finnish vehicle is operated by the municipality of Lahti. *National Motor Museum, Beaulieu*

A type OG4/9 12-ton
G.V.W. vehicle fitted
with a Gardner LK
engine used by
Nelstrop and Co. Ltd,
of Stockport

Lord Black, with a
model of the A.E.C.
'Matador' vehicle. On
the wall is a portrait of
Lord Brabazon of Tara.
The Commercial Motor

opposite top
Thames twelve-seater
bus, 1961. This model is
based on the 15-cwt
chassis and powered by
a 1703 cc OHV-engine
driving through a
three-speed gearbox.
*National Motor Museum,
Beaulieu*

opposite bottom
Leyland Super Comet
with Scammell
frameless CO_2 tanker,
1962. *National Motor
Museum, Beaulieu*

Scammell Constructor 6 × 4 wrecker/recovery vehicle with Mann Egerton 10-ton crane and Scammell Mountaineer. *National Motor Museum, Beaulieu. (Courtesy of Scammell Lorries Ltd, Watford)*

Thornycroft Mighty Antar lorry, 1962. *National Motor Museum, Beaulieu*

Leyland Scammell articulated lorry with hopper body, 1962. *National Motor Museum, Beaulieu*

Austin and Morris tractor unit, 17-ton gross train weight, 1963, powered by 5–7 litre diesel engine, five-speed gearbox and type 16802 two-speed axle. *Austin Motor Company Ltd*

Thames Trader 7½-ton 4 × 4, 6 cubic yard tipper, 1964
National Motor Museum, Beaulieu

A Type CC.6–7/25 1964 low-line crane carrier for cranes having a capacity of 20 to 25 tons

Scammell six-wheeled, twin-steer articulated lorry, the Trunker II, 1965. *National Motor Museum, Beaulieu. (Courtesy of Scammell Lorries Ltd, Watford)*

One of six type 6E6/22 six-wheel cargo trucks supplied to the Ministry of Defence in 1967

Ford Transit van, 1969. The picture shows a van, complete with instrumented dummy driver, in a 30 m.p.h. collision with a 20-ton concrete block as part of a programme of crash research. *National Motor Museum, Beaulieu*

Ford 28-ton D1000 articulated lorry powered by a V8 diesel at Southampton docks, 1969. *National Motor Museum, Beaulieu*

the firm established by Mr A. P. Hammond at Newmarket, were operating profitably, although the railways opposed them whenever possible. There was no doubt in the minds of trainers that the advantages of sending their horses by road were inestimable. Train journeys were not only tedious but highly strung thoroughbreds did not take kindly to being shut up in an often darkened box whilst their train shunted and jerked, rushed noisily through tunnels and was passed by other thundering railroad giants. At least one Derby winner was only boxed onto his train at the eleventh hour by the brute force of some dozen men, and many trainers complained that their horses arrived on racecourses after long train journeys having lost weight and condition. To be fair to the railways, however, many of their horse 'Specials' from Newmarket and other racing centres were organized with the utmost efficiency. It was understandable, therefore, that they were reluctant to accept the challenge of those who applied for licences to transport bloodstock by road.

Less serious is the story of an elderly lady who lived near Lambourn. Short-sighted and hard of hearing, she stopped a horse-box under the impression that it was a bus. The driver and the groom realized her error, but thought it would be a piece of harmless fun to open the door and let her in beside the horses. When she discovered that her travelling companion was a horse she collapsed in terror!

7

By the mid 1930s it had become obvious that the development of road transport had not only revolutionized the method of distribution of goods but had also profoundly affected industrial production owing to the practicability of transporting machinery of immense dimensions by road. Such machinery had been beyond the capabilities of the railways who could only transport it in bits and pieces for erection at its ultimate destination. Much of the credit for improving upon this state of affairs was due to the world-famous company, Pickfords, whose history began in the seventeenth century when Thomas Pickford, who owned a stone quarry on the Cheshire–Derbyshire borders, obtained a contract from the Government to supply stones for road-mending in the Macclesfield area. For this purpose he used a team of packhorses, thus providing the derivation of the modern packhorse symbol used by Pickfords. In the seventeenth century the packhorses, often carrying loads of about 700 lb in double panniers, were escorted by mounted men armed with blunderbuss, pistol and cutlass as protection against footpads and highwaymen. These security men were often in league with the footpads – with the inevitable result that the packhorses were relieved of their burden! One significant factor originating from these robberies is the present day law of common carrier making the carrier the insurer of the goods he transports. In 1777 Matthew Pickford introduced his Flying Wagons for the conveyance of passengers and goods from London to Manchester, the journey taking four-and-a-half days – accidents excepted! The shrewd Matthew Pickford also envisaged the advantages of transporting goods by canal, purchased a fleet of canal boats, and arranged for his wagons to meet the canal boats at given points. So successful was his business that by the time of the Napoleonic Wars he was able to offer the Government the use of 400 horses, fifty wagons and twenty canal boats. The advent of the railways was also used by Pickfords to their advantage. They lent their clerks to the railway companies to explain the system of freight charges, accounting and clerical procedure, and provided demountable railway containers. These containers became the forerunners of the rail-container system, and were operated from the depots in London and Manchester. In 1834 Thomas Carlyle, writing from Chelsea to his mother in Dumfriesshire, stated: 'Pickfords are the most extensive and the most punctual carriers in the world. In less than a fortnight after you give it to the steam people the barrel (if nothing happens to it) will be sitting safe here. . . .' Pickfords' business flourished, due largely to their initiative and enterprise. The evolution of motor transport did not catch them unawares, and they followed the experiments of the pioneers of the new industry with the keenest interest. In 1905 Pickfords bought eleven steam wagons manufactured by S. Hindley and Son of Dorset. These machines ran on iron wheels with iron tyres and hauled iron-wheeled trailers, and supplemented Pickfords' existing fleet of Puffing Billy and traction engines. Three years later the company purchased their first petrol-driven vehicle – a two-cylinder James and Brown lorry. It was used to carry linen from St Bartholomew's Hospital in West Smithfield to a laundry in Swanley, Kent, but did not prove satisfactory due to mechanical faults. Undeterred, Pickfords bought two Commer cars and a fleet of six 5-ton Commers, fitted with pre-selective gears. In 1910 two Daimlers and eight Thornycroft vehicles were added to the fleet. Pickfords' engineers were in constant communication with those experimenting with the improvement to fuel, vehicle lighting and tyres for it was vital that they used the most up-to-date machines to carry their loads speedily and efficiently. During the First World War a fleet of fifty Fodens was acquired, and these steam engines gave valiant service. Two significant events in Pickfords' history were their link with Carter Paterson in 1912 and their association with Hay's Wharf in 1920 caused by Hay's Wharf's interest in their meat carrying business. Thirteen years later the four major railway companies, with newly granted power to operate road services, took an equal interest in both Hay's Wharf and Carter Paterson. An illustration of transport progress made over the centuries is the fact that when in the Middle Ages a huge gun was delivered to Constantinople it required 700 men to move it. In 1930 the same gun was moved to the Tower of London by four Pickford employees!

In November 1937 the bi-annual Commercial Motor Show was held at Earls Court. During the previous two years Britain had to a great extent climbed out of the trade depression which had bogged her down in the early 1930s. The commercial vehicle industry was booming, with larger and more powerful vehicles being manufactured. Vehicles were also becoming safer, and in some instances cheaper in price. The fly in the ointment was still the Road and Rail Traffic Act of 1933 by which public carriers had to apply every two years for a licence, the granting of which was open to objection from other providers of transport. The haulier was frequently put to heavy expenditure for the renewal of his licence, the right of retaliation against those who objected to his licence did not exist, and the licensing authorities had no control over other transporters such as the railways. Admittedly the railways were run to make a profit, and also there were many road haulage operators who were little more than men of straw with virtually no knowledge of their own industry, and whose charges to their customers varied in a manner which brought some sections of the industry into disrepute, but the matter was unsatisfactory. The other bugbear – overlooking the competition from the railways – was the inadequacy of the roads. Earl Howe, as chairman of the British Road Federation, made it clear that an entirely new trunk-road system was needed, with fly-over bridges, far less speed restrictions and as few intersections and bottlenecks as possible. He claimed that the opponents of such schemes based their objections on (1) the prohibitive cost, (2) the existing railway systems would be adversely effected, (3) where such schemes had been carried out in other countries it had been for strategic and not commercial reasons. He answered these points by referring to the fact that over £75 000 000 was paid annually in road taxation and in return road users were entitled to adequate roads, to the fact that many branch railway lines were uneconomic and should be closed down, and finally to the fact that the existence of a really good and efficient road system should be a vital necessity if the country in time of war had to be supplied from Western ports with every port from Hull to Southampton under aerial bombardment.

During the early months of 1939 the storm-clouds were gathering in Europe. There were those in the industry who began to wonder to what extent the supply of raw materials would become unobtainable should war with Germany prove inevitable. Many of the basic materials used in the manufacture of a commercial vehicle came from Canada, from British Guiana, Mexico, the Argentine and Brazil. Germany had attempted, not with complete success, to become self-sufficient, and although she had produced a form of synthetic rubber she had failed to find a substitute for other vital materials. Gas was being used instead of petrol by many German vehicles which had been modified for this purpose, whilst battery electric vehicles were also being introduced.

War was declared on 3rd September. Within a month the *Athenia* had been sunk, air raids were made on Britain and the Nazi–Russian pact was signed in Moscow approving the partition of Poland. As the British war machine lolloped into action, Ernest Bevin, general secretary of the Transport and General Workers Union, stated that he was gravely concerned at the attitude adopted towards road transport by those in authority. He sensed that there was insufficient appreciation of the crucial part that road transport must inevitably play in wartime, and feared that the Government mistakenly believed that the railways alone would see the nation through. Petrol rationing was virtually forcing long-distance transport off the road, and Bevin warned that in his opinion there might be insufficient lorries at the docks to unload the ships if commercial vehicles were restricted to local transport. He also warned that a direct consequence of petrol rationing would be the discharge of commercial vehicle drivers whose services would not be available at some future critical moment. The critical moment that he had in mind was if the armed services claimed the use of almost all available railway stock and equipment to meet their needs, and the commercial vehicle industry had been immobilized. Then there would not be sufficient transport of any kind to clear food and raw materials from the docks.

By the autumn of 1940 Ernest Bevin's warning had been justified. There was a dearth of vehicles, the railways were loaded beyond their capacity, and hundreds of thousands of tons of commodities of all kinds awaited conveyance from the docks to their ultimate destinations. Sugar was at Bury St Edmunds awaiting transport to London, whilst rubber and aluminium in London was vitally needed in munition factories in the Midlands but could not be transported as there were no available vehicles. The port of Bristol was desperately short of transport of any kind, due to drivers being called up for military service. A ban on the distribution of new vehicles to hauliers made the situation worse. The antagonists of road transport based all their arguments upon one premise – fuel must be conserved in wartime. They overlooked the fact that without adequate road transport supporting the railways the movement of supplies could come to a grinding halt.

One of the essentials during the war was the avoidance of breakdowns, the minimizing of crashes and the speedy clearance of roads after accidents. Fodens used a six-wheeler carrying a powerful crane and equipped as a workshop for this purpose. The breakdown van had a deservedly high local reputation, and was so popular at Fodens that each crew of a driver and mate manned the vehicle for only a month before another team took over. On one occasion the salvage vehicle extricated an eight-wheeler of twenty-five tons gross weight which had crashed through a hedge after bursting a tyre. On another occasion a corporation steam-roller broke a vital casting and entirely blocked an already congested main road. Although the incident occurred fifty miles from Sandbach, the rescue vehicle was driven to the scene and within an hour had cleared the highway and towed the offending steam-roller back to its depot.

A few weeks before news was received of the defeat of the German armies at El Alamein in 1942, an unusual event took place in London when, at the invitation of the president of the Institute of Transport, the Henry Spurrier Memorial Trust Deed was formally handed over to the Institute. The Deed had been drawn up with the intention of dedicating a large sum of money the income from which was to be used for the promotion and encouragement of study and research in every subject connected with the development of road transport in all its aspects. This was to be carried out by establishing Henry Spurrier Memorial Scholarships and arranging Memorial lectures. The chairman of the Trust was Edward Shrapnell Smith, who handed the Deed to the president of the Institute at a luncheon to mark the occasion. Amongst the guests was Aylmer Liardet, managing director of Leyland Motors, who payed tribute to Henry Spurrier, whom he described as 'a great man and a great friend who was thorough in everything that he did and had the courage of his convictions'.

Throughout the war many of the leading commercial vehicle manufacturers switched to the production of war weapons and machinery. Morris Commercial Cars Ltd built six-wheeler cross-country load carriers and gun tractors, many of which were used in the North African campaign. During 1942 and 1943 fewer wheeled vehicles were produced as the production of Crusader tanks was stepped up. The factory at Adderley Park supplied Bofors mobile guns, field artillery tractors, anti-tank portees and units for the Morris armoured light reconnaissance cars. The first Crusader tank built by Fodens left Sandbach in October 1940. There were 1400 employees at the Foden words who patriotically worked non-stop to produce a tank every day of the week for every week of the year. Fodens also produced tough reliable W.D. vehicles, many of which were lost in Greece. An ex-Foden employee serving in the Army wrote: '. . . We got out of Greece, but we had to leave our Fodens behind. It was a heart-breaking sight to see these grand vehicles go over the cliffs to be smashed to smithereens on the rocks below. However, Jerry didn't get them, and that is the main thing. . . .' By Christmas 1941 the factory was producing 60000 shells a week, many of them assembled by the girls who took the place of those men who had been called up. Before the war was over, an experimental department was created at Fodens under the guidance of E. Twemlow to attempt the production of a new two-stroke engine. Many problems had to be overcome, including difficulties with cylinder-head valves and piston rings, but ultimately these problems were solved and a smaller engine produced which proved of outstanding merit for the Royal Navy and other navies throughout the world.

Meanwhile at Dennis Brothers' Guildford factory the monster Churchill tanks were assembled. It was Ministry policy to adopt a group system of manufacture, the bare hulls being built by one manufacturer, the twelve-cylinder engine by another and the offensive armament by another. Many of the tanks, when finally assembled at Dennis Brothers, were tested on ground near the Bagshot road with the local inhabitants deafened by the roar of the guns. After a German armoured fighting vehicle had been captured in North Africa it was brought to the Guildford factory for detailed analysis. It was discovered that the vehicle embodied several novel technical details including driving and steering on all of its eight pneumatic-tyred wheels.

At Leyland, on the instructions of the Ministry of Aircraft Production, part of the company's foundry capacity was diverted to the production of a cast-steel 250 lb high-explosive bomb. Within a year bombs of a 1000 lb type were in production. In the dark and depressing days at the end of 1941 when the sinking of the *Repulse* and the *Prince of Wales* heralded the fall of Singapore, the Russians had retreated to within fifty miles of Moscow, and the Americans had suffered the ignominy of Pearl Harbour, Leylands were concentrating on the production of Covenanter, and later Churchill, tanks. In November 1939, at the instigation of the Ministry of Supply, Leylands began to build a tank factory. Shortly after completion part of the new factory was badly damaged by enemy action. The following month they were approached by Vickers Armstrong Ltd to supply the final-drive unit for the Valentine tank, and produced more than 2000 of these units. Within eighteen months Vauxhall Motors and Leylands had entered into a contract for Leyland to manufacture the final-drive unit for the Churchill tanks. The first deliveries commenced in April 1941. Before the end of the war Leylands had built upward of 25000 engines, including those for the Matilda tanks. Parachute supply droppers and Double L Sweep units were also built. Amongst the wheeled vehicles manufactured were Beaver Eel semi-armoured vehicles for aerodrome defence which had been ordered by Admiral Sir E. R. Evans – Evans of the *Broke* – in the fearsome days after Dunkirk. These vehicles were designed, approved and delivery commenced within ten days of the distinguished Admiral's visit to the Leyland factory. At the end of the war, Leyland, in collaboration with the War Office, held an Open Day where an exhibition of all their war products was displayed.

During the war years the lot of the road haulier became increasingly more difficult. In March 1944 a letter written to the editor of *The Commercial Motor* summed up the feelings of many frustrated and disillusioned hauliers:

As the wife of a 'small haulier' I am more than anxious for the future of my husband's business and I wonder how much longer the agony will continue. . . . We are not the only ones who are facing elimination as in every trade today the small business man is being pushed around and it definitely implies that some of us have got our ideas of freedom and democracy slightly mixed with Hitler's doctrine of 'strength dominating weakness' and to which doctrine we, the British people, are supposed to be very much opposed.

Because we happen to be 'small' people does not necessarily mean that we are weak ones. We have worked hard for years and have been an asset to the country. What's more, we do not need, nor do we intend, to be bullied and squeezed out of our rightful business. If freedom is to be granted to only the few, then by all means let the chosen few fight Hitler and his gang. Control has become an ugly word in our everyday life, and one usually associates it with the end of things and, whilst we appreciate the necessity of conserving all scarce commodities, there is no need to use this power whatsoever to eliminate all the 'small' people for the benefit of the bullies and grabbers of all trades. . . . Prior to my husband's entry to the M.O.W.T. Scheme, although he was regularly employed on long distance traffic of great urgency, he experienced great difficulty in obtaining sufficient fuel, and on several occasions he was forced to obtain substantiation of the urgency. This meant losing time in order to approach the group organizer (who was also a haulier) and the sub-district office, where, to my own knowledge this application was not agreed to.

The group organizer was always airing his opinion about the days of the small haulier being numbered, and he took a great interest in our traffic. It may intrigue some hauliers to know that he is now operating over 60 miles with a non-controlled lorry, and what is more, on exactly the same work that was so difficult for us to do when we were in his group. Yet here we find ourselves controlled, doing the same journey, same job, same war, but not at the same rates of pay. . . .

Time marches on, and whilst the railways are still of great service, road transport has proved more efficient, so why should the railways have any advantage over us? As road transport is a closed industry, surely there will be enough work for all, besides this, to whom do the roads belong? If they are not for our benefit, why should we pay rates and help to keep them repaired? I can only hope that the 'small traders' will make a great effort to fight this great monopolistic menace, if they do not, they are not only helping to eliminate themselves but they are letting down every individual man and woman who is fighting and dying for freedom and democracy. Freedom has only one meaning . . . and we do not want to emerge from this terrible war to find that we can no longer think for ourselves, also to find that while we have been away the people whom we trusted have just used the war to drive finance into their own channels.

The plea of the road haulier's wife was not a cry in the wilderness, for there were many others who thought along the same lines. Mr William Foden took the view that the removal of the initiative from the hands of the individual Briton – as it would be if the Government took control of business – would result in Britain quickly becoming decadent and losing its present high standard as one of the leading nations of the world. He pointed out that when the war was over Britain's manufacturers must compete in the world's markets, and for this it was imperative that there was efficiency and a high quality of goods. Businesses must be run on the most effective lines which would necessitate control by men thoroughly experienced and with a personal incentive to produce goods at prices that would secure trade and bring a reasonable profit to shareholders.

In April 1944 Frederick Simms died at the age of eighty-one. Born in Hamburg of English parents, his life spanned the era which saw the birth of the motor car and two world wars in which war vehicles designed by him played a prominent part. In 1915 he had offered the War Office a machine which he called a Motorpedo, which was an electrically operated armoured explosive conveyor on tracks which could be steered from a distance by cable or wireless and exploded at any previously determined moment. A man far in advance of his time, his contribution to the motor industry was inestimable.

A month after Simms's death Mr P. J. Noel-Baker, Parliamentary Secretary to the Ministry of War Transport, opened a debate in the House of Commons on the subject of transport under wartime conditions and government control. In the opinion of several onlookers Mr Noel-Baker, who was presenting that part of the Civil Service estimates which came within the jurisdiction of the M.O.W.T., glossed over the true state of affairs with great political skill, and painted a far more rosy picture of the situation than he should have done. Later in the debate, Captain Gammans, speaking on behalf of the road hauliers, came much nearer the truth when he said: 'These men, who set themselves up in business by their thrift, initiative and hard work, have seen their businesses disappear. They have given up their lorries, and have gone into the pool, and they are wondering what is to happen to them after the war. Some tribute might have been paid to the grace with which they did it . . . one hears of many cases of inefficiency, of a woeful waste of transport and of not too comfortable conditions for the men who drive the lorries. . . .' Captain Gammans was followed by Captain Strickland who said that the less the State interfered with industry the better, and an example of the inefficient working of the State in a great industry was their handling of the administration of the roads. Before the debate, which covered far too much ground, including shipping, the Merchant Navy, canals and railways, ended, Mr Noel-Baker did, however, make one important announcement as to the future. 'We intend to make motorways' he promised Captain Strickland. If there was one feature of the debate which was crystal clear it was that the road transport industry had no one of sufficient knowledge and ability in the House of Commons to present their hopes and fears with lucidity and without fear of contradiction. The majority of Members in the House appeared to have little knowledge of the subject and even less interest in it.

Months elapsed and still the Government took little or no action. An application for certain public service vehicles to be increased to a new limit of eight feet in width was refused on the grounds that the roads were inadequate. Despite the requests for information on the future of the roads from the British Road Federation the Government were vague in their replies and dilatory in their answers. Mr Noel Baker claimed that 'experimental lengths of motorway' would be built – but no action was taken. The County Surveyors Society and the Institute of Municipal and County Engineers recommended 1000 miles of new motorways, but their recommendation went unheeded. As the war drew to a close, the outlook for road hauliers was gloomy. Goods vehicles of over three tons were still restricted to a speed limit of 20 m.p.h. and there seemed little likelihood of this restriction being lifted.

Churchill's Caretaker Cabinet, formed in May 1945, was succeeded by Clement Attlee's Labour Cabinet three months later. The promises of the Labour Party in their General Election Manifesto appealed to many of the voters, who included 2 000 000 Servicemen and women voting by special air post and proxy. Soon after the Election, Attlee wrote: 'The Labour Party came to power with a well-defined policy worked out over many years. It had been set out very clearly in our Election Manifesto and we were determined to carry it out. Its ultimate objective was the creation of a society based on social justice, and in our view this could only be attained by bringing under public ownership and control the main factors in the economic system. Nationalization was not an end in itself but an essential element in achieving the ends which we sought. Controls were desirable not for their own sake but because they were necessary in order to gain freedom from the economic power of the owners of capital.' Nationalization and all its implications thus became a reality. By Christmas the massive operation of demobilization had commenced, with thousands of soldiers returning to Civvy Street with their demob suit, a shirt, two collars, two pairs of socks, one pair of shoes, a hat, a tie and a pair of cufflinks. Sadly, they found that life in peacetime was in some ways as harsh as that of the war years. Drink was scarce owing to a lack of bottles in which to put wine and spirits, and cigarettes and sweets were in short supply.

Many road hauliers were appalled by the thought of the possibility of the nationalization of their industry. They referred to the petrol restrictions during the war which proved that the Ministry of Transport knew little of the practical aspects of the industry and the services that it rendered, and to the disasters of the Chartered Fleet scheme and the H.N.T.P. To add strength to their comments they pointed out the immense undertaking which was successfully operated by experienced road hauliers during the worst months of the Blitz when damage to the railways and the docks made the efficient use of road transport imperative. The Road Haulage Organization, set up by the Government, was severely criticized for the control that it imposed, and the possible administration of the road haulage industry by the Civil Service scorned. It was suggested that the Labour Government and the T.U.C. had little appreciation of the issues involved if the road transport industry was nationalized, nor had they more than an inkling as to the cost of taking over the third largest industry in the kingdom. In November 1945 the Hauliers Mutual Federation in assocation with the National Conference of Road Transport Associations, organized a meeting at Caxton Hall which was attended by more than three hundred hauliers. Opening the proceedings, the chairman, Mr E. B. Howes, chairman of the Hauliers Mutual Federation, made it clear that in his opinion the Government did not have a mandate to nationalize the industry. In the course of his speech he stated that the cost of road transport under government control was immeasurably higher than it was in the hands of private enterprise. This knowledge came from a comparison of times taken for carrying out specific movements of traffic. A further point which he stressed was the refusal of Mr Shinwell, Minister of Fuel and Power, to allow any more petrol to operators in the road transport industry, although millions of gallons were being freed so that the pooling of retail deliveries could be abandoned. It seemed that he did not intend the industry to find its feet in the aftermath of the war. Before ending his oration the chairman warned his audience that should there be a strike of employees of nationalized transport then the industry would be paralysed and its commerce brought to a standstill. At the present time such a calamity was unlikely for the industry was divided into separate compartments who were not likely to strike in unison.

The chairman was followed by Major Sir Malcolm Campbell, who began by mentioning that he had spent the past five years in the Army, and thus had a particularly close acquaintance with bureaucracy and its methods of operation. He believed that the Government's proposal to nationalize transport was a terrible thought, for State administration of industry meant stagnation, the filling up of forms, the obtaining of permits, exasperation and inefficiency. In a rhetorical speech he asked his listeners if it had been the genius of governments who had built up the finest system of transport in the world. The answer to that was decidedly no.

When Captain Gammans, M.P., rose to address the hauliers he was given an ovation, for he was acknowledged to be one of the few members of the House of Commons who appeared to be interested in the future of the transport industry. He too issued a warning which he spelt out in no uncertain fashion. He insisted that the industry must contact the general public and let them know how the nationalization of transport would affect them, and how it would harm them. He claimed that the nationalization of the Bank of England and Cable and Wireless had apparently upset no one, and in consequence the people raised no objection because they saw no threat to their freedom. In his opinion as soon as the railways were nationalized they would begin to lose money, and the Government would use the power that it has gained by nationalizing road transport to close down that industry in its efforts to bolster up the railways. He made his audience laugh when he continued: 'I suppose that when we come to the end of life's journey we shall be driven off to the cemetery in a government hearse supplied by the Ministry of Works and Buildings, encased in a utility coffin provided by the C.W.S. or with O.H.M.S. on the bottom of it, and assisted by a working party from the Board of Trade. . . . It was the great voyagers of discovery of the Elizabethan century and their successors who founded the British Empire and gave to our small island the highest standard of living in Europe. If Sir Stafford Cripps had been President of the Board of Trade at the time of Queen Elizabeth we should have become about as prosperous as the Eskimos, and it is to that level that he and his friends will soon reduce us.'

Other speakers heaped on their antagonism to nationalization. One suggested that the slogan 'You will be sorry if they nationalize this lorry' be stuck as a sticker on every commercial vehicle. Another claimed that nationalization and government control of transport would create the biggest monopoly in the country. One of the final speakers summed up succinctly when he stated that natonalization was a confession of weakness, a lack of faith in the ability of man to manage his own affairs. It was the exalting of the bureaucrat over the worker who devoted his life to his own business. On this note the meeting would have ended if it had not been announced to the astonishment of many hauliers that a Labour Member of Parliament had been listening to the speeches. He was invited onto the platform, and immediately expressed his view that much of what he had heard was totally untrue. He claimed that the British electorate had voted the Labour Party into office knowing full well that nationalization was the principal plank in its platform. He added: 'If you are under the impression that we have no experience of road haulage or passenger transport, all I can say is that you are living in a fool's paradise. In the past you have cut one another's throats. In many cases you have paid rotten wages.' Much of the remainder of his speech was drowned in shouts of derision, as hauliers protested that their businesses were not for sale.

Within two months the British Road Federation, in conjunction with the Road Haulage Association, had issued a statement against State control of the road-haulage industry. Amongst points stressed were the belief that the Government did not have a mandate to nationalize, the conviction that the industry was not a monopoly and that 'its conversion into a huge State monopoly, with all the inevitable weakening of the responsibility for decisions on the spot, the red tape, and impersonal control from Whitehall would be an act of political folly from which even the most rabid advocate of wholesale nationalization would be wise to refrain'. The faith in the efficiency of the industry, and the present excellent relationship between hauliers and their drivers must be maintained. In regard to this last factor there had been a statutory control of hours of work since 1930, and the Road Haulage Wages Act of 1938 had established a central wages board which had resulted in all wage negotiations being settled satisfactorily – even during the war years.

There was no doubt that the hauliers were united in their protests against the threat of nationalization. In an open letter to Mr Herbert Morrison a member of the M.I.T.A. wrote:

There is nothing in the world to compare with British justice, in which even the poorest individual is entitled to be represented. Might I inform you that, according to the English dictionary, the definition of justice is given as 'quality of being just – integrity – impartiality'. Can you honestly apply any of these definitions towards your intentions of nationalizing the transport industry?

Do such intentions represent a true example of British justice, when the defendant in the case is not even called upon to state his case and defend his rights? . . . Has it ever occurred to you that, during the period of your party's campaigning, you were subjected to a good, clean healthy competition? This you later admitted. Does not this fact mean or convey anything to you? What would have been your reactions had the members of the National Government had the power to retain their seats without the public being given its freedom of choice?

Might I ask you why all shopkeepers are not being incorporated into the Co-operative movement which is the 'apple of the Socialist Government's eye'? Is it because the task is too great, or would it be nearer the mark for me to say that the people would not stand for it? Good faith counts for everything. Let not your Government fail, therefore, in its responsibilities to a worthy and trusting people. There is still time to make amends.

Drivers from all over Britain were also against State control, and *The Commercial Motor* ran a prize competition for drivers to express their views. First prize was won by Lance-Corporal Murphy, who wrote:

We drivers have no doubt that nationalization will prove detrimental to an industry built up from one man carriers to the present thorn in the side to our railways. Having spent fourteen years on long-distance heavy lorry driving, most of which has been trunking, I may claim to represent the view of the majority.

We are accorded more freedom in our work than are any other works people, due in a large part, to the trust put in us by our employers, for once we are away from the depot we become our company's representative, and by the exercise of our skill and conscientiousness we determine the success or failure of the venture. On the handling of our vehicle depends our own livelihood, for a badly driven lorry is soon off the road and this is a luxury that no haulage concern can afford. Small wonder, then, that the lesser concerns encourage drivers with monetary rewards in the shape of bonuses, and by the paying of the full rate when the vehicle is laid up. Perhaps they find the man a job in the yard when his machine is off the road for some reason or other. The larger concerns cannot do this, but a good driver can always be sure of a job while there is a wagon loaded, and the relationship between man and employer is very close. This had to be, for it was only in this way that most transport businesses were built up.

With the possible advent of a great government concern this is lost. One becomes a number in a book, all individuality being lost. The man who has no loyalty abuses his vehicle and is, in fact, a bad workman. Nevertheless he has equal status and receives the same wages as the man accustomed to drive as if he owned the vehicle and worked for himself.

Surely the tendency would be to lower the very high standard already set, and proved by six years of strikeless striving and overcoming immense difficulties during the war. As for the M.O.W.T., under its auspices, what originally was three trips to Bristol per week became one return trip in five days. Need I say more than this, that to teach the Government our business would prove far too costly.

Points from other letters included: 'I have an employer whom I know and can trust. If this hideous system be passed into law I will never know whether I am doing right or wrong when under the control of Civil Servants. Fellow drivers, wake up and get this monster put down while there is time.' – 'As I see it, if the Government takes over road transport, many hundreds of thousands of transport workers will be no more than soldiers. There will probably be uniforms and military discipline . . . it will be the end of the road transport motto "Swift service with civility". . . . The Government fleets would be standardized in makes and types, and the size of a tradesman's delivery van might be limited to one ton. This would certainly mean putting some heavy vehicle makers out of business.' – 'The majority of the men dream of a glorious existence – a forty-hour week, a Labour Government which is going to spoon-feed them and cut down their milage per day, in fact enlarge the indulgence now enjoyed through the machinations of the M.O.W.T. By the latter I mean the privileges which have been enjoyed under the Road Haulage Organization. My dreams are somewhat of a different nature. I see convoys with many leading hands, and hostels where you draw your blankets, and meal tickets to be handed in, probably in a disused barracks or vehicle depot. . . . I for one refuse to be led up the garden path strewn with flowers, the name of which is nationalization; it will surely land me in eternal damnation.' – 'We have had enough experience of how government-controlled jobs were run during the war – how time and money and paper were wasted through lorries running empty on long distances. I used to do aerodrome work, and have also transported big guns behind my lorry to various depots. If the people knew how time and money have been wasted they would cry out with shame at officialdom. At one time the Government compelled us, in certain cases, to have gas producers. Look how much money was thrown away on that stunt . . . nationalization of road transport will mean dictatorship and more unemployment.'

Despite the worry of the road transport industry over the threat of nationalization, the year 1946 was a landmark for the industry, for it was considered Jubilee year. In February the Daimler Co. Ltd gave a lunch to mark the celebration of its Golden Jubilee. In replying on behalf of the guests, Sir George Beharrel, of the Dunlop

Rubber Co., referred to the recent salvage drive which had brought to light a ledger entry of 1896 showing the supply of Dunlop tyres to the newly formed Daimler Co. Three months later the company founded by John Thornycroft celebrated a similar Jubilee. The previous year a Thornycroft vehicle which had been first exhibited at the Crystal Palace Motor Show of 1896 won first prize at the Veteran Car Club Rally for the oldest vehicle to arrive at the Rally under its own steam.

In August the S.M.M.T. organized the Motor Industry's Jubilee Cavalcade in London. More than 400 vehicles, some of them veterans of the nineteenth century, were displayed in Regent's Park. The earliest machine was a Grenville steam coach built in 1875 which could carry four passengers and a man to attend to the boiler. Another interesting vehicle was an Austin ambulance which had ben captured by the Germans at Dunkirk, recaptured in the British advance of 1944 and subsequently returned by Field Marshal Montgomery to its makers. The parade of the vehicles was attended by the King and Queen, who saw Bedfords, Guys, Commers, Scammells, Seddons and Fodens drive past. A few weeks earlier Fodens had pioneered a new media for the commercial vehicle in-dustry when they had resourcefully had a film made showing the manufacture of vehicles at Sandbach. The film also showed various types of lorries performing varied and difficult tasks – with the Foden band providing background music.

Less than a month after the successful Jubilee parade news was received from Paris of the death of Jules Albert, Marquis de Dion, at the age of ninety. As a wealthy young aristocrat, but never an engin-eer, he began experiments in the early 1880s when he took George Bouton into partnership. The skill of Bouton, allied to the financial support of de Dion and his social influence, resulted in the two men successfully pioneering the motor industry throughout Europe. As a member of the French Parliament, and a co-founder of the Auto-mobile Club de France, he became a spokesman for the future of petrol-driven vehicles in an era of doubt and apathy.

Before the end of the year the Transport Bill was on the statute book. The commercial vehicle industry was still convinced that it was a monumental threat to its liberty and expressed its fears in no uncertain terms. The managing director of the British Electric Traction Co. wrote: 'The Labour Government, put into power by a minority of the electorate, proposes to make one man – the Minister of Transport – a virtual dictator over all inland transport (except for aviation) and over the destinies and livelihoods of one million men and their families. . . .' The chairman of the Yorkshire West Riding Area Traders Road Transport Association wrote: 'The general inference that I draw from the Bill is that, whereas transport has always been the servant of industry, it is going to become merely the servant of the State and will lose its close relationship with the productive capacity of industry. Nationalization could not come at a worse time. It threatens to cripple industry when the utmost elasticity and efficiency in transport are needed for the export drive which is so vital to the nation's economic position. It is my view that no State-controlled system of transport can have the flexibility of transport run by private enterprise.' Another writer, possibly thinking back to the music-hall jingle of the turn of the century:

> What is a Communist, one who hath yearnings,
> For equal division of unequal earnings.
> Bungler or blunderer, or both, he is willing
> To pocket your pound and give you his shilling.

stated: 'The Bill is just another measure introduced to implement a state of Communism under the less offensive title of Socialism. The objective is to eliminate individualism and replace it with State ownership and control of all the essential requirements of the community. The price which the politician offers to pay for this control is the provision of the fundamental amenities of life to all members of society. The price the community pays is the unconditional surrender of its individual liberties. . . .'

In March 1947 a motion was carried in the House of Commons by 289 votes to 150, applying the guillotine to the proceedings on the Bill in the Committee, Report and Third Reading stages. The reason given by the Lord Privy Seal for this action was to avoid an autumn session. Such a statement was greeted with fury and derision from the Opposition benches. Mr Churchill flayed the Government – but without avail – and the House became a scene of pandemonium for several minutes. The end of the battle came five months later when the Bill received the Royal Assent on 6th August. It was a time of despondency which was not alleviated by the August sunshine enjoyed by holiday-makers. The winter of 1947 had been one of the coldest in memory, and had been followed by the most appalling floods. The Prime Minister announced that the American Loan, expected to last until 1950, was running out rapidly, and the Chancellor of the Exchequer informed the nation that the convertibility of sterling into dollars was temporarily suspended. So too were foreign travel allowances. The nation became 'Austerity Britain' with the Minister of Fuel, Hugh Gaitskell, supporting a campaign for 'Four inches only in the bath' and Dr Edith Summerskill suggesting the delectability of 'snoek'.

The trade unions were becoming known as 'The fourth Estate of the Realm' and boasted 'We now have an open door in relation to all State departments'. In 1939 the unions had been represented on twelve government committees. By 1947 this had increased to almost sixty. One of the few bright and happy highlights for the nation was the marriage of Princess Elizabeth to Prince Philip of Greece in November. During the next two years British railways were nationalized, as were the gas industry and the electricity industry; Mahatma Gandhi was assassinated; the Berlin air lift took place, and the new State of Israel was proclaimed. In London a young comedian named Danny Kaye took the town by storm, as did the musicals *Annie Get Your Gun* and *Oklahoma*. It was as though the world was shaking itself free from the aftermath of the war years and was determining the future course that it intended to take – even if it was a course which was singularly lacking in any sort of appeal to some of its inhabtiants.

In the world of the commercial vehicle industry the year 1949 was considered a year of great achievement. The output of commercial vehicles was the highest ever, exceeding 200000 and thus doubling the output of the last pre-war year. Manufacturers such as A.E.C., Fodens, Leyland and Vauxhall all contributed to the record rate of production. The increased production was due in part to improved methods of production and efficiency resulting from new factory layout, but equally to the determination of the entire industry to beat previous achievements. Increases in steel allocations were also a contributory cause, even though they fell short of the manufacturers' requirements. One of the brakes on the industry was the penal level of taxation, which meant in general terms that the purchase of new plant and equipment had to be financed by raising additional capital instead of out of ploughed-back profits. As an overseas visitor remarked, 'You can't tax a country into prosperity'. Another brake on full-scale production was the Government's refusal to modify the Construction and Use Regulations which compelled manufacturers to build to one standard for the home market and another for overseas. There was little doubt that the manufacturers were at loggerheads with the Government over the number of vehicles to be exported. Despite a dock strike, and complications caused by restrictions on currency and import permits, the commercial vehicle manufacturers had exported vehicles valued at more than £36 000 000 in the first ten months of the year. This record achievement should have been acclaimed, but instead the manufacturers were rebuked by the Ministry of Supply for having exceeded the quota laid down for the home market! To add force to the rebuke the manufacturers were informed that control of sales by licensing would be imposed unless home deliveries were reduced, and exports increased. Such rebukes did nothing to cement relations between a patriotic and hard working industry and those who issued edicts from the remoteness of Whitehall.

The April 1950 Budget of Sir Stafford Cripps failed to improve the relationship. The tax on petrol and oil fuel was increased by ninepence a gallon, whilst his 33⅓ per cent purchase tax on goods vehicles in order to divert production to exports was received with mistrust. Although the S.M.M.T. put forward their view that it was essential to have a strong home trade as a basis on which to build an export trade, their advice went unheeded. The disillusioned industry were reduced to believing that the Chancellor was not prepared to encourage the aggrandizement of the commercial vehicle industry, and was prepared once again to consider its interests subservient to those of the railways. who were demanding through the British Transport Commission an increase of 16⅔ per cent in railway freight charges.

When the Budget was discussed in the House of Commons Mr Winston Churchill attacked the Government and claimed that the imposition of a heavy purchase tax on vans and lorries was a direct attack on the economy and efficiency of production and distribution, and also that the tax on their fuel was designed to force the travelling public to use the nationalized railways. Mr Douglas Jay, Financial Secretary to the Treasury, said that the real purpose of the fuel tax was to assist the economy in a dollar commodity, and that of the purchase tax to restrain excessive investment and to encourage exports. The industry found it difficult to accept the truth of his assertions. Mr R. A. Butler, in his summing up, remarked that there must be an understanding between road and rail, and that vindictive measures in the Budget did little towards such understanding. His impartial judgement fell on deaf ears, although at the end of July it seemed that some progress was being made towards this understanding when the British Tran.port Commission issued a statement of policy setting out the part that road transport would play in the future of Britain's nationalized transport system. The intention was to develop road and rail as complementary agents. Long-distance smalls and wagon-load traffic on trunk routes would be passed to the railways. The Road Haulage Executive would provide collection and delivery services for the railways and would carry on cross-country routes much of the traffic formerly handled by the railways. At a press conference announcing details of the new policy Lord Hurcomb, chairman of the British Transport Commission, said, 'There will tend to be a redundancy of vehicles', which did not please every member of his audience.

In September the fifteenth Commercial Vehicle Show was held at

Earls Court. One of the most notable features of the show was the fact that several manufacturers had departed from the conventional practice of adopting an underfloor position for the power unit. Fodens had mounted the engine of their new model at the rear of the chassis in a vertical position. To some extent the interest shown in the exhibition by overseas prospective purchasers was not as great as had been hoped, but, as Lord Nuffield pointed out, the majority of overseas visitors were serious buyers as opposed to those prompted by curiosity. Where the home market was concerned many prospective purchasers, considering themselves hamstrung by the purchase tax regulations, were deciding to make their existing fleet of vehicles last for as long as possible. Some of the leaders of the commercial vehicle industry were unhappy at the results produced by the show and thought that the money used to stage it could have been better spent in an overseas exhibition. There was also disagreement as to how frequently the show should be held in future years. Sir Patrick Hennessy was in favour of every two or three years. Lord Nuffield felt that another show in 1953 would be soon enough whilst Mr E. R. Foden and others believed that 1954 or even 1955 would 'fill the bill'. There did seem, however, a unanimous feeling that certain aspects of the show, such as the presentation of the vehicles on the stands, could be improved on future occasions. Six months after the Motor Show it was announced that Leyland Motors and Albion Motors had amalgamated. Albion were Scotland's last remaining motor manufacturers, but leaving sentiment and nostalgia aside, the merger seemed a logical step to take. Years previously the Commer and Karrier concerns had become part of the Rootes Group, which had more recently acquired Tilling-Stevens Ltd and Vulcan Motors Ltd whilst Crossley, Maudslay and A.E.C. had amalgamated to form the A.C.V. Group. It seemed that the commercial vehicle industry was closing its ranks.

In the General Election of 1951 the Conservative Party were swept back into power – even though they secured less votes in total than the Labour Party. Amongst Mr Churchill's new Cabinet were Sir Anthony Eden, Harold Macmillan and R. A. Butler, men dedicated to denationalization wherever possible. By July 1953 the steel industry had been denationalized and the steps to denationalize the road haulage industry were far advanced. Eighteen months later the twenty-five-mile radius limit imposed seven years earlier was removed. Statistically, this enabled 63 000 commercial vehicles, most of them on A licences, to become available to undertake long journeys. At the time that the restriction was removed the chairman of the R.H.A. wrote:

. . . We have suffered more than our fair share of political interference. It has shackeld the growth of the road haulage industry over the past five years. During much of this time the country's production and prosperity have been on the increase. Hauliers have played some part in helping this development, but time and time again have been prevented from doing more by the arbitrary ban on their movement outside a radius of twenty-five miles.

Now comes the opportunity for steady expansion of road haulage in its service to trade and industry. The effect of the relaxation may not be immediately apparent, for most hauliers are at present fairly well occupied on work arising from the country's improved economic condition . . . thus for the first time since before the war the road haulage industry can resume its interrupted course. Once more the trader can have the choice of a number of specialized services, not only for his local deliveries, but for the carriage of his goods to and from all parts of the country. . . . It is not unreasonable to hope that before long the industry will have regained all the ground lost in the past few years. If trade and industry make their opinion plain no question will ever again arise of politicians deliberately creating obstructions to the efficient development of road transport merely for political ends. . . .

Within twelve months Sir Winston Churchill had resigned, to be succeeded as Prime Minister by Sir Anthony Eden, Clement Attlee had resigned and accepted an earldom, and Hugh Gaitskell had become the elected leader of the Labour Party. In the autumn Budget restrictions were introduced to curb spending on consumption and investment, and certain sections of the commercial vehicle industry found that it was becoming more expensive to finance the purchase of vehicles. The British Road Services, with more vehicles at their command than was originally envisaged in the Transport Act of 1953, were in a strong position, in consequence of which the owners of some 2000 long-distance heavy vehicles found that their free enterprise was being challenged by the 5000 vehicles of B.R.S. With considerably less financial problems than private hauliers, B.R.S. were able to order 125 Octopuses from Leyland Motors Ltd, all of them eight-wheelers for 24-ton loads. It seemed that the might of the B.R.S. fleet was steadily outnumbering the aggregate number of its rivals.

In January 1953 the Marine Sales division of Fodens – who had been developing their own two-stroke engine for both automotive and marine and industrial use – received an unusual letter which proposed that Fodens might be interested in a project concerning the crossing of the Atlantic in an open boat! The author of the letter, Cecil Harcourt-Smith, was an ex-Royal Navy officer who had served from 1925 to 1929 as A.D.C. to the British High Commissioner in Egypt and from 1930 to 1938 had been British Representative to His

Highness the Khedive of Egypt. Harcourt-Smith discussed the project at Fodens, pointed out that both joint managing directors of Fodens owned boats powered by Foden marine engines, and suggested that if a double crossing of the Atlantic was achieved for the first time by a small power craft it would bring prestige for Britain and make the Americans somewhat envious! Before approaching Fodens, Harcourt-Smith had looked around for a suitable craft, and had found a boat which in his opinion would be suitable. The Padstow lifeboat *Princess Mary*, which had been built in 1929, was due to be sold out of service. Fodens agreed to the project, the lifeboat was bought by Harcourt-Smith and was sent for reconstruction to Messrs Tough Bros of Teddington. Months later, having shed her funnel, and with other details of her superstructure simplified, she emerged as M.Y. *Aries*, a craft 61 feet long with a 15 ft beam and a displacement of 45 tons. Below deck her new engines were space savers and her generator provided power for lighting, cooking, and battery charging.

Amongst the crew of five was eighteen-year-old David Foden, elder son of joint managing director Ted Foden. David, after leaving Cheltenham College, was undergoing his National Service training with a unit of the Royal Artillery at Oswestry. His commanding officer gave him leave of absence, believing that the spirit of adventure should be encouraged. M.Y. *Aries* took twenty-eight days to cross the Atlantic from Dartmouth to New York and nineteen days to complete the return journey. In approximately 1500 hours 8448 miles were covered and for twenty-two days on the run from Dartmouth to Bermuda the engines were run non-stop. On 10th August M.Y. *Aries* returned in triumph to the Thames, where she was greeted in traditional fashion by the sirens of the river traffic.

After the excitement of the Atlantic crossings, made to seem more adventurous after the comment of a friend, 'I would not cross the Atlantic tourist in the *Queen Elizabeth*', David Foden completed his military service, ultimately becoming a subaltern in the 33rd Parachute Field Regiment. Later he worked for a year at Gardner's Patricroft works before joining the sales side of Fodens. His younger brother Edwin also worked for twelve months at Gardners and had a year in Australia prior to returning to work at Sandbach. David and Edwin's cousin, William Foden, son of R. G. Foden, had been born in New South Wales in 1929. Educated in England, he spent a year in the Foden workshops before returning to Australia. He came back to England in 1949 and a year later joined the sales side of the company.

In July 1956 Fodens celebrated their centenary, for in 1856 Edwin Foden had become indentured to Messrs Plant and Hancock. Ten years later he became a partner in the firm, whilst in 1868 his son William was born. At the time of the centenary celebrations William Foden, in his eighty-eighth year, was still the governing director of the business, having been managing director since his return from Australia in the 1930s until two decades later, when he handed over the reins of office to his son J. E. Foden, to R. E. Foden and to E. Twemlow whose father had married Miss Fanny Foden, a daughter of the founder of the firm. Whilst he was in Australia, William Foden, with considerable foresight, had written home recommending that the company should make oil-engined vehicles with Gardner power units. The new models were designed from scratch as a diesel, for until this moment in their history Fodens had never invaded the sphere of petrol-driven engines.

In the year 1868 Lawrence Gardner, describing himself as 'L. Gardner, Machinist', had set up his business in the cellars of a house in Upper Duke Street, Manchester. Young, ambitious and with a wife and eight children to support, he was willing to adapt his skill as a machinist to a variety of work. He made machine parts, machine tools, parts for sewing machines, and milling and cutting machines. With a growing reputation he found that the cellar workshop was inadequate for his needs, and moved to larger premises in nearby Cornbrook Park Road. His eldest two sons, after winning scholarships (established by Sir Joseph Whitworth), joined the business, as did his other four sons once they had learned their trade as engineers. In consequence Gardners was essentially a family business even though there were twelve other employees. In 1890 Lawrence Gardner died at the age of fifty, leaving the thriving business to his widow. The following year the works was again moved to larger premises in Lund Street, where eighty men were on the pay-roll. A range of dynamos, the heaviest weighing three tons, were manufactured and a new profitable product undertaken – the production of dentists' chairs. More important, the firm agreed to manufacture a patent hot air engine designed by A. E. H. Robinson, which had initially been described as 'a useful and thoroughly good motor for driving small machinery'. Lawrence Gardner's sons, intelligent and perspicacious, realized that their future lay in the development of the internal combustion engine. They had followed the careers of Lenoir, Nicolaus Otto, and Robert Bosch with keen interest, and were convinced that the demand for internal combustion engines would steadily increase. Gardners produced their first oil engine in 1894, and gradually produced a range of engines from $\frac{1}{2}$ h.p. to 25 h.p. These machines sold well, although it became apparent that the virtually non-existent sales force of Gardners was not equipped to cope with the orders from customers. Agents were appointed, including the newly formed partnership of Edward Norris and Charles Henty, whose father was the famous author whose historical novels had thrilled Victorian schoolboys. The increased prosperity of the business necessitated yet another move to larger premises. Three acres of land were bought on the edge of Chat Moss, between Manchester and Warrington, and workshops covering half an acre built. In 1898, three years after the move, the Gardner partnership was changed into a limited liability company, in order that additional capital could be raised to finance the expansion. The Gardner brothers typified the industrious far-sighted engineers whose ingenuity and mechanical skill were to bring world-wide renown to British engineering in the years prior to the First World War. At the end of the nineteenth century they claimed: 'The immediate future holds within its palm developments in power production dreamt of only by a few, but which will exert an enormous modifying influence upon all grades of human life and energy.' By the year 1900 Gardner engines were turning dynamos, lighting theatres, powering wireless sets, pumping water, compressing air and driving ships. Their customers included the War Office, the Admiralty and the India Office. A decade later they were selling engines in every corner of the globe, and the engines were being made at the rate of one an hour, with a thousand employees working for the company who were virtually self-sufficient from the moment that the raw materials arrived at the factory until the finished engine was ready for sale. Quality was of overriding importance, and they were justifiably proud of their great reputation. For some years Gardners had been experimenting with a range of two-stroke semi-diesels derived from the engines of Ackroyd Stewart, who had patented an engine in which the fuel was injected into air compressed in the cylinder by a stroke of the piston. Gardners always felt that their engines were no more than first cousins to those of the illustrious Dr Diesel, for in his engines fuel was forced into the cylinder head by an air blast, whilst Gardners used mechanical injection.

Gardners, like many other engineering firms, were affected by the economic depression of the 1920s, and by 1924 the work force had been reduced to 420. However, the new experimental laboratory, built in 1919, continued to develop new ranges of engines, and it was decided to redesign the entire range to produce compression ignition engines which were true diesels as opposed to semi-diesels. The new engines started from cold on compressed air and developed full power immediately. Many years later Sir Harry Ricardo, speaking at a meeting of the British Association, praised Gardners when he stated: 'Gardners in 1928 and 1929 achieved what no other firm in the world had succeeded in making, viz. a small high-speed open-chamber

Ford 22–24 ton DT1700 tipper, 1970, powered by 185 b.h.p. V8 diesel engine. *National Motor Museum, Beaulieu*

With three historic Foden vehicles in the background, the Foden Motor Works' Band pose with their conductor for many years, Rex Mortimer, in the company's museum during October 1972. In the background, from left to right, the Foden 7-ton steam wagon 'Pride of Edwin', a Foden steam traction engine 'Pride of Leven' and the 1931 Diesel No. 1

Left Lord Stokes. *British Leyland*

Opposite top Lord Nuffield. *National Motor Museum, Beaulieu*

Opposite bottom Foden Universal six-wheeler, 1974. The heavy duty three-axle chassis is primarily intended to accept tipper bodies and is powered by a turbo-charged 12-litre Cummins 220 engine

Cruising at high sustained speeds is one of the major demands of operators today. Taking a stretch of motorway in its stride is this S80 fibreglass cabbed Foden 4AR6/34 powered by a Rolls-Royce Eagle 220 Mark II engine. It is towing a York Freightmaster semi-trailer

Foden S80 fibreglass cabs being assembled at the company's Sandbach, Cheshire, works. The cab is designed to meet the demand for improvements in driver comfort and ease of control and maintenance. Only the front grill panel need be raised for routine service checks

engine with a multiple orifice injector which was consistently reliable. The Gardner engine stood in a class by itself thanks to the meticulous skill and care in its design and to superlative workmanship.' The greatest success of the Gardner L2 engine, which was first shown to the public at the 1929 Marine Show at Olympia, came as a result of the visit to the exhibition of Mr Trevor Barton of Barton Transport, Beeston, Nottinghamshire, who was so impressed by the engine that he went home with the germ of an idea for its future use. The consequence was that early in 1930 an engine was delivered to his garage, installed in a single-deck Lancia bus and put on trial. A month later the bus went into service to become the first vehicle engine conversion from petrol to diesel with a British-made diesel and the first all-British diesel engine to be used in a road vehicle. It was a unique landmark in the history of the commercial vehicle industry, and was elaborated upon in November 1930 by Mr Tom Gardner, managing director of Norris, Henty and Gardners Ltd, who sent out a circular letter regarding L2 engines for Road Transport.

The purpose of this letter is to try to give you an idea of what has been done and what is being done with regard to the application of L2 engines to road transport.

In the first place the L2 engine was designed chiefly for marine propulsion, electric generator sets, ships' auxiliary sets, light rail locomotives and such like. It was not intended for road transport work; nevertheless it is being extensively used for this purpose. Its first application was due to the initiative of Messrs Barton Transport Ltd of Beeston, Notts., who after inspection of the engine on test, decided that, notwithstanding its weight and relatively low speed, it was suitable for bus work. They took a 4L2 engine away with them on 28th February 1930 and installed it in a single-decker bus. After some preliminary running the bus was put into regular service on 12th March 1930 and has run ever since in a most convincing style.

After doing 20000 (twenty thousand) miles we persuaded Messrs Barton to let us have the engine at our works for testing, inspection and calibration. We put the engine on test just in the state in which we received it, and found everything to be in perfect order, the consumption of fuel being 1 per cent up. We then stripped the engine, and calibrated the parts with most satisfactory results. After which we reassembled the engine without effecting any repairs beyond that of rubbing in the valve seats. The bus has now run nearly 40000 miles and is still running satisfactorily. Messrs Barton have taken, in all, four engines including a 5L2.

The first bus attracted visitors from all parts of the country with the result that we became inundated with enquiries and orders.

The following are among the most notable installations.

Leeds Corporation. Double-decker bus by Crossley Motors Ltd. with 6L2 engine. Put into regular service on 24th September 1930 and is doing 950 miles per week.

Sheffield Corporation. A duplicate of the Leeds Corporation bus; just about to go into service.

Manchester Corporation. A triplicate of the Leeds Corporation bus; not yet delivered.

Walsall Corporation. A 4L2 in one of their existing single-decker buses. Has been in service for a few weeks.

The following manufacturers of lorries have installed our engines in their lorries.

H. I. Thornycroft & Co. Ltd. One 6L2 in a lorry of gross weight 15½ tons. Has been running since the beginning of August 1930.

Walker & Co. Ltd. Pagefield Lorries. Two 4L2 and one 3L2.

Talbot Serpell. 4L2 delivered 26th August 1930.

Tilling-Stevens Motors Ltd. Electric transmission 4L2 engine.

Karrier Motors Ltd. 6L2 delivered 10th September 1930; now in service.

Gray Motors Ltd. 6L2 not yet delivered.

In addition to the above, quite a number of existing lorries of various well-known makes have had their petrol engines replaced by L2 engines. The firm who initiated this business of conversions is Frank H. Dutson (Leeds) Ltd of Leeds, who are experts at the job and have ordered 36 engines for this purpose, 4L2, 5L2, and 6L2. All the 'conversions' in actual service are giving the utmost satisfaction. We ought to add that in all cases of conversion, the existing gearboxes have been used without modification.

Wallis & Steevens Ltd. have ordered 19-3L2 engines for road rollers of which they have taken 12.

On the whole, we have by now gained a good deal of experience of road transport work, experience of a very pleasing character. First of all we learn that, without exception, the drivers of the L2 vehicles prefer them to petrol vehicles on account of their great flexibility of drive and the power of acceleration. One of the great differences between the petrol and the oil engine is that in a petrol engine, as the revolutions fall so does the torque, but in the oil engine, the torque remains practically the same at all speeds. Another thing which the drivers comment upon is that the L2 engine is much cooler running than the petrol engine, which adds materially to their comfort. It is a significant fact that in none of the L2 vehicles is a fan used with the radiator. This is not surprising because the thermal efficiency is so much greater than that of the petrol engine, the heat to be dissipated by the cooling water being less than half that of a petrol engine.

One of the points where the L2 engine scores over other high-speed diesel engines is the starting by hand which is our standard method of starting. To start, all the cylinders are entirely relieved of compression; this enables the engine to be cranked round by the hand starting handle with the greatest ease. As soon as the flywheel has attained a sufficient speed, say 130 r.p.m., the decompression lever of the nearest cylinder is thrown out of action when the engine instantly begins to work; the other decompression levers are then turned out of action, putting in work the remaining cylinders.

We have fitted a few engines with electric starters at special requests, but, so far, not a single vehicle engine. In all these cases hand starting is preferred.

At home there is a general wakening up to the fact that the diesel engine is arrived for commercial vehicles. The Press, public and technical, are giving great prominence to it. All this is of course attracting other makers to the field and no doubt we shall have in due course more rivals than at present. Whatever be the outcome, the fact will always remain that the L2 was the first British engine to enter the field of road transport.

Once those associated with road transport appreciated the immense advantages of the diesel-engined vehicle which could run twice as far on diesel oil as on petrol, the demand for Gardner engines became greater than ever. Commercial vehicle manufacturers realized the importance of fitting Gardner engines to their latest models, and at the 1931 Commercial Motor Show at Olympia Guy exhibited their Goliath 11-ton rigid six-wheeler equipped with a Gardner 6LW engine.

Fodens, who had taken delivery of their first Gardner engine earlier in the year, showed a 6-ton lorry powered by a 6L2-type engine. These vehicles were the forerunners of a vast number soon to be put on the market, for both manufacturers and users appreciated the reliability of the engines which allied to their economy made them universally popular. The one prejudice which had to be overcome was the belief that oil engines were expensive to maintain. This prejudice arose from diesel engines previously imported from the Continent, which, in the words of Sir Harry Ricardo, 'for their noise, smoke and smell were intolerable, whilst their heavy maintenance costs went far to counter their advantages in the way of fuel costs'. The prejudice was soon overcome, conversions to diesel came on apace, and the L.M.S. Railway Company converted ninety-one vehicles to diesel in 1932 – the cost of conversion being between £300 and £350 for each vehicle. Some employers were worried that their drivers would have difficulty with the new type of engine, but their fears proved groundless. By the beginning of 1932, Karrier, Scammell, Guy, Foden, Albion, Daimler, Dennis and Atkinson were but some of the commercial vehicle manufacturers who offered their lorries with a choice of their own petrol engines or Gardner power units. Since the revolution in the commercial vehicle industry caused by the development of the diesel engine, the word Gardner has been synonymous with superlative workmanship.

Also superlative was Foden's Brass Band which for more than half a century had been deservedly famous and had won prizes worth more than £35 000. In October 1953 the band won the Daily Herald

National Contest at Earls Court, their tenth championship victory. Two sons of the much beloved Fred Mortimer, who had died in June, contributed to this triumph, Harry Mortimer as conductor, Rex as bandmaster. Amongst the victorious Foden band were Arthur Webb, who had been solo horn player for forty-three years, and Fred Sowood, bandsman for forty-five years. Fodens Band had played in France and Belgium during the V-Day celebrations, and later in the week had returned to London to appear on a TV programme compèred by Wilfred Pickles. One of their most outstanding international victories had been at Hillegom, Holland, in 1954. The band, consisting of skilled craftsmen, fitters, platers, joiners, pattern-makers and bodybuilders, were to gain the highlight of their career when in 1973 they were invited – and accepted – to play at Annabels in Berkeley Square, London, which is the most fashionable night club in Europe! The band also played an important part in the Foden centenary celebrations, which included a parade of veteran vehicles, a firework display and a feast for 5000 guests, mostly Foden employees and their families. To add a touch of authenticity to the proceedings, some of those men taking part in the veteran parade refused to shave until the celebrations were over, in order that they should look more like their ancestors!

The year 1957 was disastrous for Britain. It opened with the Suez crisis and the consequent fuel shortage. Anthony Eden resigned and was replaced by Harold Macmillan. Not until May was the petrol rationing which had been imposed on 17th December 1956 lifted. In September the bank rate was raised to 7 per cent and before Christmas ninety people were killed in a railway accident at Lewisham. Such tragedies in a year of gloom did nothing for the commercial vehicle industry, whose production programme was dislocated. Export sales were lost through currency restrictions and at home hauliers lost business through lack of fuel. A strike of provincial bus company workers in July made matters worse and only the ingenuity of hauliers prevented a complete standstill. However, the year did prove that the commercial vehicle industry could withstand a barrage of economic difficulties beyond their control and remain intact.

Six months later the industry hoped for some form of relief in the Budget produced by Mr Heathcote Amory, but their hopes were dashed. There was no reduction in the fuel tax, nor was the 30 per cent purchase tax removed from goods vehicle chassis.

In June 1958 the first official rally of the Historic Commercial Vehicle Club was held at the Spurrier works of Leyland Motors. Sir Henry Spurrier was president of the Club and Mr J. E. Foden a vice-president. Amongst the exhibits was a 1916 Foden 3-ton steamer, a 1923 Rolls-Royce with a lorry body for garage use and 571000 miles behind it, and a 1927 Leyland Lion.

For the next year the possible return of a Labour Government who might restore road haulage nationalization hung like the sword of Damocles over the heads of the leaders of the commercial vehicle industry. The victory of the Conservative Party for the third time in eight years in the autumn of 1959 and their majority of over 100 in the House of Commons diminished the threats of further nationalization, and the hauliers breathed a sigh of relief. What was rapidly becoming the foremost of their thoughts was the future of motorways. the first of which from London to Birmingham was to be opened before the end of the year.

The new Minister of Transport, Ernest Marples, was a man of dynamic personality, with far-sighted ideas for the future. During the immediate post-war years he had built Marples, Ridgeway & Partners into a vast concern with contracts in every part of the world. Sheer hard work, allied to business acumen and initiative, had been the cornerstones of his success. Marples was Member of Parliament for Wallasey, a constituency once held by Lord Brabazon of Tara, a man who became a legend in his lifetime. Whilst still a schoolboy at Harrow, he had written a treatise on mechanically operated inlet valves, and as a nineteen-year-old had acted as Charles Rolls' mechanic when he raced in Ireland. He held the first pilot's certificate granted by the Royal Aero Club, and in 1909 won the *Daily Mail* prize for flying a circular mile in an all-English machine. A member of the Royal Yacht Squadron, a low-handicap golfer, described by Roger Wethered as 'the best bad golfer in England' and an experienced Cresta Run tobogganist, Lord Brabazon became chairman of A.V.C. on its formation in 1951. Few have crammed their life with so much fulfilment both at work and at leisure as this great man.

The A.C.V. group, consisting of A.E.C., Crossley, Maudslay, Park Royal Vehicles and Thornycroft, typified the consolidation of commercial vehicle manufacturers into units of greater size through amalgamation. The Maudslay Engineering Company at Alcester, Warwickshire, had been founded by the brilliant inventor of the slide-rest and screw-cutting lathe, Henry Maudslay, who had been born in 1771. His great-grandson R. W. Maudslay created the Maudslay Motor Company in 1903, and began building lorries and buses. The reputation of the company brought them many orders in the early years of the youthful commercial vehicle industry. Equally renowned were Thornycrofts, who had begun experiments with steam vans in their Basingstoke factory in 1896. One member of the Thornycroft family was the distinguished sculptor Thomas Thornycroft, who was responsible for sculpting the massive figure of Boadicea and her chariot which had been commissioned for erection near Westminster Bridge. The sculptor's Chiswick studio was commandeered for the building of steam wagons, once Boadicea had departed!

Crossley cars and commercial vehicles had been manufactured at the Errwood Park works at Stockport since 1906, the same year that the Vanguard Company opened a factory at Walthamstow, with the principal intention of overhauling buses used on the London streets. In June 1912 the Associated Equipment Company was formed at the behest of the London General Omnibus Company and commenced the manufacture of virtually all London buses, including the legendary 'B'-type' bus. The Vanguard Company was the nucleus of A.E.C., who in 1926 moved to a 63-acre site at Southall. In 1948 Crossley and Maudslay were acquired, and the name of the group changed to Associated Commercial Vehicles Ltd. A year later Park Royal Vehicles was added to the group which incorporated Thornycroft in 1961. Throughout these years the dominant personality was William Black, born in 1893. After serving his apprenticeship with Vickers Ltd he became works manager of Vickers at Crayford in 1924. Ten years later he was appointed director and general manager of Park Royal Vehicles, and before the outbreak of the Second World War was managing director, in addition to being appointed a director of A.C.V. In 1957 he became managing director of A.C.V. and chairman seven years later. Created a Knight Bachelor in 1958, he was made a life peer in 1968. President of the Society of Motor Manufacturers and Traders Ltd in 1953, he was a member of the Queen's Award to Industry Advisory Committee 1965–72. A man distinguished both for his ability and his appreciation of the problems of others, his life spans more than sixty years in the commercial vehicle industry. He has seen the industry grow to manhood and fulfilment, and has always believed in its future despite the occasional pessimism that he received from others. When he became managing director of A.C.V. and chairman of A.E.C. he thought that it was incumbent that he got better acquainted with his colleagues and fellow workers. He therefore attended several social gatherings, including the A.E.C. annual sports meeting. As he walked round the ground, chatting to all and sundry, he found himself talking to a complete stranger to whom he addressed the question, 'Do you work here?' 'Yes,' came the reply. 'I am an engineer on the assembly line.' By this time Black was bursting to tell the stranger who he was, so he added the information that he too was an engineer. 'Well,' came the prompt reply, 'if you work here, get out – there's no future for the likes of us!'

In 1954, whilst Minister for Transport, Ernest Marples visited the Finals of the Lorry Driver of the Year Competition. The competition had originated in 1951 when the Coventry Road Safety Officer, Mervyn Miles, had presented Safe Driving Awards at the Standard Motor Company. One to whom Miles made an award was Jack Patience, a Transport and General Workers shop steward and a member of the Coventry Road Accident Prevention Council and the Coventry Courtesy Club, who for many years had organized car rallies. Patience suggested to Miles that commercial lorry drivers should be included in these rallies, but after discussion it was agreed that the lorry drivers would be 'too professional'. The chairman of the Accident Prevention Council, Bob Brain, was consulted and wisely proposed that a separate competition be held for lorry drivers. The first competition was confined to the Coventry area, but in 1953 there were so many entries that the competition had to be held on two consecutive Sundays. In 1954 Coventry was joined by Portsmouth and the competition was christened 'Lorry Driver of the Year' at the suggestion of Raymond Baxter of the B.B.C., who for two seasons acted as Clerk of the Course and was responsible for much of the national advertising. Enthusiasm for the competition spread like wildfire and in 1957 M. Gilbert Lesage, a representative of Les Routiers, the French organization for lorry drivers, invited the English committee and the winning drivers of the year's competitions to meet their French counterparts in a special contest at Versailles. The contest was an outstanding success, but due to lack of finance was not repeated. In the early years the finals were held at a variety of places, including Fort Dunlop and Coventry Airport, but from 1965 have been held annually at the Royal Naval base at Bramcote in Warwickshire. Until 1965 the national competition was organized by the Coventry Road Safety Office, but the administration became so great that they were forced to relinquish the task, which was taken over by *The Commercial Motor*, who had been involved in the competition from its inception. Although Coventry gave up the work involved in organizing the competition, Bob Brain, who had always insisted that the true purpose of the competition was road safety, continued as national chairman until 1970 when he was made honorary life president together with Mervyn Miles. In 1968 his achievements on behalf of the competition were rewarded by an M.B.E.

Qualifications for entry to the competition include the essential factor that the entrant earns his or her living by driving a freight vehicle, is not an instructor, and has not had a serious licence endorsement nor blameworthy accident during the previous twelve months. Although the competition has always been open to women drivers it was not until 1973 that a female became a National Class

A Champion. Champions have, however, had a variety of jobs. One winner was a china clay haulier in Cornwall, another carried eggs in Ulster, and a third drove a petrol tanker in the Scottish Highlands. There are forty centres as far apart as Aberdeen and St Austell, where preliminary heats are held prior to the National Final, the entire competition being administered by the national secretary A. D. Wilson, whose office is in the Commercial Motor department at Dorset House, London. Prizes each year are awarded by many companies associated with the commercial vehicle industry, including Michelin, Shell Mex, Chrysler United Kingdom, Tate and Lyle and the Transport and General Workers Union. There are classes for eight types of vehicle.

The four rigid and four articulated classes.

The four rigid and four articulated classes

18 Classification

Rigid Vehicles
Class A Up to and including 24 ft. overall length, over one ton **and up to 2 tons registered unladen weight.**
Class B Up to and including 24 ft. length **and exceeding 2 tons registered unladen weight.**
Class C Over 24 ft. and up to and including 28 ft.
Class D Over 28 ft.

Articulated vehicles
Class E Up to and including 40 ft. overall length, with flat or sided semi-trailers having flat or drop-frame.
Class F Up to and including 40 ft. overall length, with box or tank semi-trailers.
Class G Over 40 ft. overall length, with flat or sided semi-trailers having flat or drop-frame.
Class H Over 40 ft. overall length, with box or tank semi-trailers.

The contest consists of a road route, a written paper on the Highway Code and legal requirements of drivers, and manoeuvring tests which are devised to simulate actual driving situations which occur from time to time in reality and require every ounce of the vehicle driver's skill and ability. The accolade of the competition came in the report of the Minister for Transport Industries informal committee, published by H.M.S.O. in November 1973, which stated:

7.1   The problems of the roads and the lorries which frequent them become considerably less if lorries are driven well. Bad manners and reckless driving, abuse of the law, can do immeasurable harm to the degree of acceptance of a business activity now crucially important to our society and under the spotlight of criticism for its environmental offences. We need to raise the level of social approval for the lorry driver, who frequently receives general disapproval from the shortcomings of the few.

7.2   The Industry boasts a high degree of professionalism among its drivers, now reinforced by the law in the recognition accorded to the H.G.V. licence. In an industry which continues to grow and expand, however, there is a great need to recruit and train drivers to high quality standards if dilution of practice and behaviour is not to occur at a time when the demands of the technology of distribution and transport on the driver continue to increase (Appendix H provides one example). The issue of the supply of good drivers could become critical in the next few years. In conjunction with the R.H.A. and the F.T.A. we have recently highlighted the problem, and alerted the authorities and our own companies to the need to reinforce training investment. We also believe that the Government

153

should give stronger support to the *Lorry Driver of the Year Competition*, which has done much to keep high standards of driving competence before the driving fraternity and the public at large. Many firms insist on their drivers observing codes of practice, demand good standards of driving, and require regular medical reviews – which we recommend should be made compulsory for drivers over, perhaps, fifty years of age. Considering the miles they drive and the continued inadequacy of many of the roads over which they travel, lorry drivers have a good record, in spite of the general criticism and opprobrium they incur whenever an individual lapse occurs.

Thirteen years earlier the national chairman of the Road Haulage Association, J. B. Mitchell, stated:

Nearly thirty years ago the railways were still the predominant partner in transport, but were already feeling the effects of competition from a new and vigorous rival. For this reason, and because the railways were subject to certain restrictions from which road carriers were free, the Government thought it proper to impose some brake on the increase in the number of road goods vehicles carrying for hire or reward. There was also a widely held opinion that, apart from the possible harm that was being done to the railways, road haulage was expanding too quickly, with the result that irresponsible newcomers to the industry were unable to maintain their vehicles properly, or even to stay in business at the rates they were charging, and ended up in the bankruptcy court. Whether or not this assessment of the situation was correct it did have a considerable influence upon the Government of the time.

The creators of the licensing system must have believed also that they were acting for the benefit of traders and manufacturers, especially those who wished to carry their own goods. The ancillary user was given complete freedom to continue to operate under C licence and it was the intention that he should also have available a properly balanced and stable body of professional carriers by road and rail. The situation has already changed considerably, and is likely to change even more as the Government plans for transport take effect. The railways have long since ceased to be the dominant partner. The obvious way out of their financial difficulties is to streamline their activities so that they can concentrate on the kind of traffic which they may hope to make pay, and leave other traffic alone. This appears to be the underlying motive of the government policy at the present time, and it would obviously involve releasing the railways from any obligation to carry all the traffic that may be offered to them. Some arrangement must be made for dealing with the goods that the railways can no longer handle. The obvious alternative would be a road haulier, the very man who, of all transport operators, finds his activities at present most closely circumscribed.

. . . The Socialists have always had an eye on the possible restriction of the freedom of the C licence holder, and there seems some thought even in a section of the Conservative Party of curtailing their activities, by the institution of another tax or levy . . . it is reasonable to suggest, therefore, that the Government should look with favour on amendments to legislation which would allow existing hauliers to absorb traffic that would otherwise have to be dealt with either illegally or by the expedient of putting more C licence vehicles on the road. It is possible that the Government will take the lead in proposing such legislation, once its value and inevitability become plain . . . my own view is that the established haulier with his experience that ought to be of incalculable value to the community should be given the opportunity to enlarge his activities so as to meet any shortage of transport created by the contraction of railway activities. . . .

The words 'contraction of railway activities' received far greater publicity in March 1963 when Mr Marples told the House of Commons about the Beeching Plan for the streamlining of British Railways. He pointed out that any additional demands on the roads would be met in consequence of the extensive reshaping of the railways. Mr Marples, whose speech was given a hostile reception by the Opposition, made it clear that in the opinion of the Government the Beeching Report was a major contribution to providing an efficient, economic and well-balanced transport system for Great Britain as a whole. He added that rationalization of freight services was of the greatest importance not merely to the railway's finances but to industry and commerce. When the Opposition spokesman, Mr George Strauss, replied, he explained that as far as the Beeching recommendations for making the railways more efficient were concerned, the report had the wholehearted support of the Labour Party. But the proposals to curtail the railway services on a drastic scale confirmed Labour's worst fears. In particular they were surprised and distressed at the scant attention that Dr Beeching had devoted to the congestion of the roads.

8

The 1960s saw the culmination of the struggle between Leyland and the British Motor Corporation, a struggle in which Sir Donald Stokes was so closely involved. After leaving Blundell's School, Stokes had gone to Leyland as a trainee. Unlike so many young men who had little idea as to their future career, Stokes had always longed to make the motor industry his vocation, and had spent so much time at school poring over motor magazines that he was nick-named 'motor blokes'. Dedicated to Leylands, his flair for salesman-ship, his initiative and energy spelt success – and success which would have come sooner but for the intervention of Hitler and his Nazi war-lords. In 1945 Stokes, who had become one of the youngest Lieutenant-Colonels in the British Army, received his great chance when he was invited by Henry Spurrier – the grandson of the original Henry Spurrier – to produce a thesis on the method by which Leylands should approach the question of post-war exports. The resulting thesis was a brilliant exposition which proved conclusively that Stokes had not only mastered every aspect of the problems in-volved but also had the imagination and drive to solve them. He became the greatest salesman in Leylands' history. Years later he claimed: 'Customers don't want a lot of chit-chat. They look for down-to-earth advice based on a knowledge of the vehicle and of the economic background against which it is to be used. Engineering comes into this, of course, and so does what is generally known as "business consultancy" as well.' To some die-hard and old-fashioned Leyland salesmen Donald Stokes's methods of salesmanship seemed unorthodox, for he based his enterprising and ambitious outlook on the premise that the Leyland factory must produce the number of vehicles that he sold, whereas his predecessors had often taken the view that they could only attempt to sell the number of vehicles that the factory had produced. Such a view had no appeal for the dynamic Donald Stokes!

During the 1950s Leyland acquired two commercial vehicle manufacturers, Albion and Scammell, and before the end of the decade the possibility of acquiring Associated Commercial Vehicles (the conglomeration of A.E.C., Park Royal Vehicles, Crossley and Maudslay) had been broached. At the time nothing came of the overtures, although the directors of Leyland were anxious to expand their interests. In 1961, after protracted negotiations, Standard Triumph was added to the Leyland empire. The subsequent year there were rumours that A.C.V. might be taken over by B.M.C., but despite the fact that informal discussions were held between the chairmen of both companies, nothing materialized. Suddenly other rumours spread, implying that there had been meetings between Stokes, Spurrier of Leyland and Brabazon and Black of A.C.V. The rumours proved correct, and in June 1962 A.C.V. was added to the Leyland organization. Within months of the merger Henry Spurrier III became ill, and Sir William Black succeeded him as chairman of the Leyland Motor Corporation. For the next four years business boomed.

At the 1964 Commercial Vehicle Show a new range of trucks was introduced, designed to meet the amended U.K. Construction and Use Regulations announced in September. The range, named Freightline, comprised two·, three· and four-axle chassis for haulage, tipping and tractor applications with gross ratings from 16·32 tons. Each model featured the Leyland Ergomatic cab which could be tilted to an angle of fifty-five degrees to give instant access to the power unit. The name was derived from ergonomics – the scientific study of man in relation to his working environment. Six months later a 'gold watch ball' was held at the Tower Ballroom, Blackpool, to which all employees with more than twenty-five years' service were invited. Watches were received by 1500 long-service employees – the first one being presented to Mr Basil Nixon, who had been appointed to the board of directors in 1907 after having acted as company secretary. In 1966 Leyland Motors were among the first recipients of the Queen's Award to Industry, and Rover was merged into the Corporation.

In March the Labour Government had won a victory at the General Election and were returned to office with an overall majority of ninety-seven. Three months after winning the Election the Prime Minister, Harold Wilson, announced a six months' freeze on wages, salaries and prices. The outlook appeared bleak, but did not prevent talks continuing between Leyland and B.M.C. on the subject of a merger between the two giant companies.

Herbert Austin and William Morris had both found that the years immediately following the First World War brought economic difficulties which reduced their companies to a parlous financial state. It would not be unfair to comment that both men had enjoyed the pioneering days of the industry more than the years when the giant companies that they had created became almost unwieldy. In 1924 there was a suggestion from Herbert Austin that a merger between them might be advantageous, but Morris would not contemplate the idea, and to illustrate his rejection outbid Austin for Wolseley.

For the next decade the anchor man of the Morris organization was Leonard Lord, who in 1938 moved to Austin after differences of opinion with Morris. Such a move enhanced the rivalry between the two companies – a rivalry which was to last until 1951 when the two companies finally merged into the British Motor Corporation. In 1961 George Harriman succeeded Leonard Lord (Lord Lambury) as chairman and managing director of B.M.C. Two years later Harriman tentatively mentioned the idea of a merger to Sir William Black. The complications of such a merger with the problems of agreeing an acceptable price, and the stumbling block caused at times by a clash of personalities between some of the most influential members of both companies, resulted in almost seven years of protracted negotiations before agreement was reached. Heralded with understandable jubilation, the agreement announced, *inter alia*, that the new group would control almost 40 per cent of the commercial vehicle market in the United Kingdom.

Less than a year after the merger Sir Donald Stokes, who had been knighted in June 1965 for his services to export, spoke on 'The Future of Road Haulage in British Industry' at the annual conference of the Road Haulage Association. He pointed out that transport was the biggest individual cost item in all the manufacturing processes. Road haulage accounted for 72 per cent of all freight ton mileage in Britain as compared with only 34 per cent in West Germany. This commanding lead for British road haulage proved that British road hauliers provided a better means of transport to the user. While it would be highly inconvenient if some disaster wiped out what remained of the rail network, Britain would survive, but without motor transport the nation's economy would grind to a halt. The motor manufacturers had a huge vested interest in road haulage, with British Leyland Motor Corporation selling 34·7 per cent of the 225000 commercial vehicles sold in the United Kingdom during

1967. One of the problems highlighted in his speech was the fact that although motorways were built at huge cost, productivity deals associated with the higher permitted speeds were difficult to introduce. The objections raised to the introduction of tachographs were unbelievable considered against promises of productivity made when pay claims were entered. He suggested that in return for productivity concessions lorry drivers would demand a sophisticated lorry, comparable in comfort and performance to the motor car. Power steering, power brakes, and a driver's cabin which had excellent comfort, with visibility and handling standards at present undreamed of. At question time Sir Donald Stokes was asked if higher tax allowances to buy British vehicles were called for. He replied: 'If you do not buy British you want your head examined. If you buy American-owned firms' products, the dividends go to the United States. All you're doing is cutting your own throat and ensuring that you pay more income tax.'

In June 1964 two great men of the commercial vehicle world died: Henry Spurrier and William Foden. William Foden died in a Congleton nursing home at the age of ninety-five. A man totally devoid of pretensions, pomp and circumstance were alien to his nature and his religion. He left behind him a reputation as an upright and just Christian gentleman, endowed with the qualities of comprehension and compassion. At his funeral the cortège was led by the Foden band, whilst his coffin was borne on a high catafalque on the wagon of a 1916 Foden steam wagon named 'Pride of Elwin'. Born in the year that the Suez Canal was formally opened, he lived to see the advent of motorways and juggernaut lorries capable of carrying enormous loads at high speed. A man of vision and foresight, he took an active interest in the future of the commercial vehicle industry in general and Fodens in particular up to the time of his death. This future had been succinctly appraised by the chief designer of Fodens, J. B. Mills, in the summer of 1964 when he wrote:

Despite all the pressures and developments of alternative forms of prime mover, the diesel engine will still reign supreme because of its high efficiency and reliability. Power will increase from the present average of around 6 b.h.p. per gross ton to 10 b.h.p. per gross ton or more. This will be necessary in order to keep all road vehicles moving at a more constant speed and thus utilize the roads to the maximum advantage. The motorways will revise thinking on road speeds and schedules, and, in order to give these engines powers of 300 b.h.p. or more, highly rated types of turbo-charged machine will become pre-eminent, whilst we may see more attention to uniflow scavenged two strokes to get more power without a penalty in weight and size. . . . British heavy goods vehicles are going to get more sophisticated, but at the same time they must retain the toughness for which they have always been renowned. . . .

Fodens own renown took another step forward the following year when their band made a long-playing record under the conductorship of Sir Malcolm Sargent – the recording commemorating the distinguished conductor's 70th birthday.

A new era in the history of Fodens dawned in March 1972 when the joint managing directors handed over control of the company to their sons. The three new joint managing directors were thirty-five-year-old David Foden, son of Ted Foden, Patrick Twemlow, aged thirty-three, son of Edwin Twemlow, and forty-one-year-old William Foden, son of Reg Foden. Fodens had gone public in 1911 and by 1972 the directors and their families owned less than 5 per cent of the issued shares. Nevertheless, the pride in their family firm became the driving force for the new managing directors, just as it had been for their fathers and grandfathers. It had been suggested that on the retirement of William Foden at the age of ninety-two in 1960 a 'them' and 'us' situation had developed between the management and those employees on the shop floor mainly because of William Foden's personality and the vacuum caused by his retirement. David Foden grasped this nettle firmly when he made it clear that in his opinion a case of 'them' and 'us' did exist *but* the *'us'* was everyone at Sandbach, and the *'them'* was British Leyland, Volvo and Mercedes Benz. He added: 'We have tried to involve people in the day-to-day successes and problems of the company. That means a lot of memos go out signed by the joint managing directors. It means lots of communiqués and meetings with the employees' representatives. Of course, there is still an element of autocracy. The attitude we convey is "We are here to run the company and that is what we are going to do for the benefit of all of us".'

Within a month of taking the helm the new joint managing directors authorized a £3 000 000 production expansion programme. The result of this authorization was the building of the most modern and sophisticated heavy commercial vehicle assembly plant in Europe. After six months of intensive planning the foundations for the 3 000 000 cubic feet building was commenced in February 1973. Less than nine months later the first vehicle was produced off the line. The plant, capable of producing vehicles at the rate of three an hour, consists basically of a three-line overhead conveyor system 279 metres long. The long-term plan was to build up to 100 units a week within the 1975–6 year.

One consequence of the expansion programme was a rethink on the subject of rationalizing the range of models produced. For

A sleeper version of Foden's S80 fibreglass cab. The sleeping facilities inside the cab provide for a relief driver to sleep while the vehicle is still mobile, or, with further bunk flap pulled forward across folded seats, both crew men can sleep

6 × 4 Foden type AC29/75 tractive unit, powered by a Cummins NTC 290 diesel engine, at work on a section of the new M62 Goole motorway

Foden 6 × 6 medium mobility military vehicle. Designed primarily as part of Britain's FH70 NATO commitment, the basic chassis can also accommodate various specialist equipment and body variants. With a top speed of around 70 m.p.h. a 305 b.h.p. Rolls-Royce Eagle power unit drives through Foden's nine-speed gearbox and two-speed transfer box

Foden low mobility military vehicle. These trucks are designed to operate fully laden on both highway and unsurfaced tracks and, with the use of differential locks, performance and mobility approaches that of vehicles in the medium mobility classification. This chassis too can accommodate various types of specialist equipment and body variants

Fodens' modernization programme has created a production unit equal to the best in Europe. The production line, which is master-controlled by a computer, can produce trucks for highway or construction industry use, in a range of gross weights from 20 to 100 tons, in any required combination or sequence. *Photographed by Maurice Broomfield*

At each stage in the manufacture of a Foden component, the high precision work is carefully inspected, ensuring the highest quality control standards. *Photographed by Maurice Broomfield*

Towards the end of Fodens' production line the wheels and tyres are fitted and the vehicle rolls forward on a moving floor. The cab is fitted before the vehicle is checked, tested, started up and driven away for a detailed programme of operation and road tests on Fodens' own test track.
Photographed by Maurice Broomfield

Fodens themselves manufacture a very high proportion of the components for their trucks. Bevel pinions and gear wheels are forged, and then machined, hardened and ground in the firm's own machine shop.
This photograph, commissioned by Fodens and taken by Maurice Broomfield, was highly commended in the 1974 *Financial Times* Industrial Photography Awards presented in London on Monday, 10th February 1975

decades it had been the policy of Fodens to manufacture vehicles to each customer's exact specification and requirements. By 1973 the model range had been reduced to less than twenty-five, and Foden salesmen, having determined a customer's transport problem, suggested the most suitable model to cope with it. As David Foden explained, 'We now have a better range of trucks, fifteen tons and over, than ever before and the range was devised after a highly specialized and thorough market research job. We have a wide range of extras for every model and are still a long way from having a mass-produced truck.' He added: 'Our philosophy is still to build the best premium-built, volume produced truck in the world.'

Fodens, like other British commercial vehicle manufacturers, realized the significance of Britain's entry into the Common Market. As an initial step towards acknowledging Europe as its home market, Fodens linked up with the West German group Faun-Werke who specialized in off-road vehicles such as dump trucks and crane chassis. In Britain Foden-Faun began to import and distribute Faun products through the Foden sales organization, whilst Faun-Foden import and market Foden commercial vehicles in the E.E.C. countries. Fodens, convinced that there is no cheaper way of shifting a ton of goods than by road transport because it gives a door-to-door service, believe in the future of juggernaut lorries despite the attacks upon them from some quarters. They also believe that a 38-ton truck need not be larger or noisier than a 32-ton truck.

The entire question of the size and shape of heavy commercial vehicles of the future had been under review on the Continent for almost a decade. The problem besetting transport Ministers of the E.E.C. countries was to compromise between the French gross weight of thirty-eight tons and the Dutch gross weight of forty-eight tons. Axle loading proved another problem for it varied between nine tons in Italy and thirteen tons in France. By midsummer 1972 the transport Ministers of the Six in Brussels finally agreed that the maximum gross weight should be forty tons and the axle loading eleven tons. This agreement radically altered the outlook for British manufacturers, for the gross weight permitted by the Common Market countries was eight tons more than that permitted in Britain, and one ton more regarding axle loading. The E.E.C.'s decision to allow 11-ton axle loading immediately posed difficulties on British roads where many bridges were considered unsuitable for axle loads in excess of ten tons. Criticism of the traffic jams caused by juggernaut lorries in cities and towns grew apace, with suggestions appearing in the Press that such monster vehicles should be banned from certain roads. There were also suggestions that British commercial vehicle manufacturers should look to their laurels due to continental competition.

For years the light commercial vehicle industry in the United Kingdom had been dominated by B.L.M.C., Chrysler (U.K.), Ford and Vauxhall, whilst the heavy commercial vehicle industry had been almost exclusively controlled by Fodens, E.R.F., Seddon and Dennis. By the summer of 1971 a period of recession had set in for the heavy commercial vehicle manufacturers, made more serious as it followed a long period of expansion and success, some of it resulting from the Government's decision to introduce 'plating' and maintenance tests on lorries in 1970. The maintenance tests drastically increased safety measures, whilst 'plating' ensured the operators did not load their lorries with more than the manufacturers recommended. These measures caused many operators to replace their vehicles. World economic conditions, a cutback in capital investment by industry, uncertainty over the Government's intentions regarding future weight regulations, and President Nixon taking emergency measures to protect the dollar were all contributory causes to the recession. It was not a propitious time to have to prepare for an onslaught of foreign competition.

For seventy years British manufacturers had virtually reigned supreme in their own country despite General Motors' acquisition of Vauxhall in the mid-1920s. At a conference on the European Motor Industry, sponsored by the *Financial Times*, and held in London in October 1973, Dr Joachin Zahn, chairman of the Board of Daimler-Benz, claimed that a well-functioning European commercial vehicle industry was indispensable in supplying transport needs which – as a result of European integration – would continue to increase rather than decrease in future years. Indirectly his words were a warning that Britain must think as a European. He added: 'It must be remembered that road systems cannot be enlarged indefinitely, particularly in view of prevailing environmental standards and land-use planning which sets limits to expansion.' He forecast a rocky road for the future of the commercial vehicle industry in Europe, but declared that the lorry could not be banished from the economy. 'Its place in the future is assured as an indispensable partner for sensible co-operation with other means of transport, above all the railways. For the individual European manufacturer the road into the future will nevertheless be full of potholes, steep hills and obstacles.'

He also prophesied increased competition from new and especially non-European manufacturers, whilst at the same time the European industry's opportunities to export to third-world countries would diminish. He expected that the trend among customers would be increasingly towards large single firms or state services and that because of favourable exchange rates American and Japanese manufacturers would be competing in Europe. He continued:

If you expect me to tell you how many manufacturers there will be in 1980 or 2000 I am afraid that you will be disappointed, because I do not think much of this sort of prophecy. I believe that a concentration process such as took place in America will not necessarily take place alongside the integration of the European market, especially since, as far as I can see, the opportunities for useful co-operation have not been exhausted. In this context I should like to refer to the current extremely friendly co-operation with the largest British manufacturer who supplies engines for some of our light transport.

Referring to the future development of the European commercial vehicle industry Dr Zahn said that Daimler-Benz were already selling 80 per cent of their commercial vehicle production on the European market. By the time the company had produced its millionth diesel truck since 1945 in November 1972, they had come to regard Europe as their home market, and continued to do so, even though several large companies of international significance had announced that they intended to become more active than previously on the German commercial market. Reviewing the present status of the truck, Dr Zahn said that at the commencement of 1973 there were approximately nine million commercial vehicles registered in Western European countries, or 23 per 1000 inhabitants. By comparison the United States had 97 per 1000 inhabitants and a total of 20 000 000 vehicles, and Japan 92 vehicles per 1000 inhabitants and 10 000 000 vehicles. It was becoming clear that in future manufacturers would have not only to provide vehicles to their customers but to offer whole transport systems and help in solving customers' specific transport problems.

Fodens in the autumn of 1973 helped to solve the problems of one vitally important customer when they secured a contract worth £10 000 000 to supply the Ministry of Defence with heavy vehicles. The contract was to provide the British Army with a large proportion of its low mobility load-carrying fleet. The vehicles, to be powered by Rolls-Royce diesel engines, were based on the commercially proven Foden eight- and six-wheeler rigid chassis with the new S90 cab. The contract, equivalent to 15 per cent of Fodens output, commenced in 1974 and would be spread over three and a half years.

In January 1974 it was announced by Mercedes Benz that they intended to resume the importation, marketing and servicing of their products in Great Britain as a result of an agreement reached with Thomas Tilling Ltd who had held the franchise since the early 1960s through their wholly-owned subsidiary Mercedes Benz (Great Britain) Ltd. The reason for this resumption was Mercedes determination to get to grips with Europe's largest commercial vehicle market once Britain's entry into the Common Market had caused tariff barriers on commercial vehicles to be lowered. The entry of Mercedes as a direct competitor to British commercial vehicle manufacturers had serious repercussions both in the heavy truck sector and also in the light vehicle market. A further repercussion was added when International Harvester, the leading United States makers of trucks and tractors, successfully bid for Seddon Diesel Vehicles. The bid represented International Harvester's second attempt to establish itself in the United Kingdom truck market, for in the mid-1960s the company had established a plant at Doncaster to manufacture its own trucks. The annual output of Seddon, being approximately 2500 medium-weight Seddons, and 1500 Atkinsons, was small in comparison to that of Fiat or Mercedes Benz, but nevertheless was an important milestone in the evolution of the commercial vehicle industry in Britain, and spearheaded International Harvester's decision to become a contender for a share of the lorry market of Europe. This decision compelled the industry to appreciate the significance of the fact that only three wholly British commercial vehicle manufacturers – Fodens, E.R.F., and the British Leyland Motor Corporation – remained from the large number established prior to the outbreak of the First World War. The prosperity of the three, and particularly that of the vast conglomerate of the B.L.M.C., who were entangled with the complexities of re-organizing a vast and involved mixture of car manufacturing companies and the better organized but still complex commercial vehicle division, became of vital economic importance as the industry looked to the future. The future, however, was not to be re-assuring, The world oil crisis following the Arab–Israeli war in the autumn of 1973, the political chaos following the Conservative Government's confrontation with the major Unions and the resultant General Election and return to power of the Labour Party in the spring of 1974, heralded the beginning of a world recession which gathered momentum as the months sped by. The effects of the recession were particularly drastic in the United Kingdom. The three remaining British commercial vehicle manufacturers, already under extreme pressure from European and American competition, and hampered by the tardy reaction of the Government to introduce more favourable Construction and Use Regulations, – enjoyed by foreign competitors in their own domestic markets – were faced with the possibility of catastrophic collapse.

Before the end of the spring industrial unrest in Britain led to pickets attempting to stop lorries from entering power stations and factories. The Government's proposal to make such action by pickets legal caused a torrent of letters condemning such irresponsible action. One letter in *The Times* stated:

164

Who in this country, except the police, has or ever has had the right to stop citizens from going about their own business? Are we now to extend that right to every Tom, Dick and Harry calling himself a picket? Is a picket now to become an arm of the law, to have power to arrest? – and how, one wonders, is the stopping of lorries to be effected if the lorry driver decides he does not wish to stop? How – except by physical action of some sort against him. Will this then be legal? Will the police, if necessary, have to help the pickets to exercise their rights by forcible means?

Another letter in similar vein was from a parson who wrote: 'How convenient it would be if a parson preaching in the open air had the power to insist that passers-by stop and listen to his case. Alas! I fear that he would find himself in trouble with the Council for Civil Liberties and the Council for Individual Freedom.'

In the autumn of 1974 the question of the legality of picketing remained an ugly political thorn. The Employment Secretary, Mr Michael Foot, advocated that pickets should be given freedom from prosecution if they obstructed the highway to prevent lorries from reaching their destination. Such advocacy was diametrically opposite to the views of other leaders of the Labour Government, who considered that only the police should have the right to order a vehicle to stop. In their opinion any alteration of the law to favour pickets would increase the danger of industrial violence and add to the risk of injury to police officers. Such opinion was endorsed by the police force who believed that one of the problems, if the law was altered, would be the identification of authorized pickets with the right to

"Didn't you read? Princess Anne's passed her heavy goods vehicle driving test."

stop lorries as opposed to unauthorized trouble-makers. Such opinions highlighted the prevalent industrial unrest – unrest which could seriously jeopardize the future of lorry drivers irrespective of their political affiliations if fanned to white heat by militant Marxists and International Socialists.

The arduous working life of commercial lorry drivers had never been free from hardship, but in recent years their welfare has come under close scrutiny and been given greater priority than ever before. E.E.C. nations have insisted on a code being laid down as to working hours and conditions, whilst in Britain emphasis has been placed upon combining comfort with efficiency for drivers. High on the list of priorities for the modern vehicle are fully adjustable seats for the driver, radio-telephone link between the driver and his firm, lock-up compartments for documents and valuables, and cassette slots on the dashboard. Many drivers favour the Bostrom Viking as the ideal seat for their cab, and in Volvo lorries this is now a standard fitment. Such comfort is the right of the lorry driver, whose skill and ability is often overlooked. So too are the hazards which at times he is compelled to face. Driving a juggernaut lorry in narrow town streets can require immense expertise – an expertise frequently forgotten by those who consider such a vehicle to be a social evil. Appalling weather conditions, with snow, ice and fog, can also add dangers to his efforts to deliver his load on schedule. The hazards of his life were highlighted in June 1974 when a limpet bomb was found attached to a road tanker *en route* for Canvey Island. Whether or not the bomb had been stuck under the lorry by members of the I.R.A. is not of significance. The incident illustrated to the general public the fearsome possibilities which could occur if a large tanker carrying highly inflammable chemical or liquid gas exploded in a town or city.

Throughout the summer of 1974 the question of the future of rail and road transport again came under review: Constant references had been made to this conflict, but few had the clarity of an article by Edwin Shaw which appeared three years earlier in *Wheels*, the journal of the United Road Transport Union:

There were over one hundred railways at the start and they foolishly duplicated facilities so that traders could pillage them even more. They loved litigation and the lawyers have seen more profit from the railways than the shareholders ever did. They were busy but threadbare and unprofitable when this century dawned and with their passion for public good as opposed to their own they threw themselves into two world wars and came out practically bust financially and mechanically. In 1922 Parliament amalgamated them into four but by this time 1925 was with us and 100 years had passed. 1925 saw the serious introduction of large motor coaches and long distance lorries and private cars were going into volume production. These three unglamorous workhorses spelt the end of the glamorous but inefficient steam railways. However it took the railways and Parliament 35 years to realize this was the fact. The railways could not realize that one man driving one lorry was more efficient than a railway where it took the actions of tens of thousands to get goods moved from one place to another. The advent of the lorry ruined the admirable concept of charging on what the traffic could bear . . . it was easy to assume that road haulage was full of rogues and vagabonds and even Parliament today shows signs of anti-road bias.

Whatever this bias might be, the then Minister of Transport, Mr Fred Mulley, stated that Britain's roads would be built to a lower standard in future and were likely to become more crowded. Such a statement was not encouraging for those who believed that juggernaut lorries were the solution to all transport problems. The apparent object of the Minister's parsimony was to save money and land, but he did admit that he hoped that a network of 3100 miles of high-quality roads would be in existence by the early 1980s with particular emphasis on the needs of heavy lorries. He thought that even allowing for 'a substantial shift' of freight and passenger traffic to rail, a continuing national roads policy and programme was still necessary. The details of the Rail Bill, published in June 1974, gave an indication of the state of the railways during the next five years, and also an indication of the competition it would offer to road transport. The proposal to provide £1500 million to develop an efficient railway network, seemed to many with vested interests in road transport to imply the likelihood that directly or indirectly the railways might be able to offer freight charges at more favourable rates than could be offered by road haulage operators. Understandably, they criticized the Bill, publicly and privately. In the midst of this criticism the Minister of Transport circularized a paper which he hoped would be used as a basis for discussion by those willing to assist the Government and local authorities in deciding how the movement of heavy lorries could be made more acceptable. The number of lorries involved was approximately 534000, based on those registered in the United Kingdom at the end of 1973.

Laden Weight (tons)	Number of vehicles
$3\frac{1}{2}$–$8\frac{1}{2}$	154000
$8\frac{1}{2}$–16	245000
16–24	72000
over 24	63000

In his Foreword the Minister stated: 'I recognize that there are limits to the extent to which freight can be transferred from road to rail; my proposals in the Railways Bill at present before Parliament will help to make the maximum practical use of railways for the movement of goods. . . .' Those who studied the competition of rail and road throughout the past sixty years realized as they read these words that the problem of rivalry still existed. Fundamentally the problem had never altered, for lorries can deliver supplies to locations inaccessible to railways. Consequently the need for suitable routes for heavy vehicles is a priority which can never be overlooked, and was emphasized in the study *Living with the Lorry* by Dr Clifford Sharp, sponsored by the R.H.A. and the F.T.A. and published in 1973. The author made a systematic attempt to evaluate the damage caused by lorries under headings – noise, air pollution, road wear, accidents, vibration, delays to other road users, visual intrusion and damage to buildings. It became abundantly clear once the headings were considered in detail, that any solution would have to be assessed in terms of money available, time and general convenience, in addition to the acceptable size of juggernaut lorries. It is possible in the future that Common Market countries will insist on each nation conforming to certain specific standards for weight of vehicles; to all vehicles being driven on the right-hand side of the road; to tachographs, known in some quarters as 'spies in cabs', becoming compulsory; and to more stringent regulations being enforced regarding the power of braking systems. These possibilities, even collectively, do not outweight the most vital of all considerations for the future – whether or not monster juggernauts should be allowed to use the same roads as other motorists, many of whom are terrified by the magnitude of the gigantic lorries which at times monopolize motorways, country roads and the streets of towns and villages. This consideration is crucial, and must be resolved – for the course, direction and policy of the commercial vehicle industry depends upon the agreed and accepted solution to the future role of the juggernauts.

In Britain the early months of 1975 brought immense economic problems to the commercial vehicle industry. B.L.M.C., bedevilled by difficulties and setbacks, found themselves in a critical liquidity and profit position. The Ryder Report, issued in April 1975, proposed a capital injection into the company of £2 billion over the next eight years. In the Report it was mentioned that partly as a result of the tendency to replace commercial vehicles more frequently due to stringent vehicle legislation, it seemed probable that the demand for heavy trucks within the United Kingdom might increase by 30 per cent during the next five years. Overseas demand was seen as good – especially in countries which were oil producers (Iran and Nigeria) or had good access to favourably priced oil (Turkey) and were expanding rapidly. Fodens were also having problems, and were obliged to call for Government help when their cash crisis became equally critical at about the same time as the distress of B.L.M.C. became apparent. The problems facing Fodens and B.L.M.C made it abundantly clear that the role of the independant manufacturer in the world motor industry was becoming more difficult on a day to day basis. The precedents set by the nationalized industries of the Continental countries, and the enormous conglomerates of the United States (such as Ford, General Motors and Chrysler) were causing the highly resilient but smaller British survivors to be put under intense pressure. This pressure was aggravated by the impossibility of funding the capital needed for future expansion from a collapsing stock market.

Despite internal and external economic problems, British industry has constantly shown its apptitude and ability to overcome difficulties, partly through its resilience and partly through dint of its inherent strength of character. Therefore the years ahead can be faced with confidence by the commercial vehicle industry whose initiative and enterprise have conquered adversity in times of peace and times of strife, and whose growth throughout the past century has been a major factor in the industrial history of modern Britain.

Selected Bibliography

ANDREWS and BRUNNER, *Life of Lord Nuffield*, Blackwell, 1955
ARMYTAGE, W. H. G., *Social History of Engineering*, Faber and Faber, 1956
BAILEY, Leslie, *Scrapbook 1900-1914*, Muller, 1957
BIRD, Anthony, *Roads and Vehicles*, Arrow Books, 1969
CORNWELL, E. L., *Commercial Road Vehicles*, Batsford, 1960
DENT, H. C., *Milestones to the Silver Jubilee*, Halcyon, 1935
ENSOR, R. C. K., *England (1870-1914)*, Oxford University Press, 1936
JEFFREYS, Rees, *The King's Highway*, Batchworth, 1949
KLAPPER, C. R., *British Lorries 1900-1945*, Ian Allen, 1973
LAMBERT and WYATT, *Lord Austin the Man*, Sidgwick and Jackson, 1968
MILNE, A. M., *The Economics of Inland Transport*, Pitman, 1955
NOBLE and JUNNER, *Vital to the life of the Nation*, S.M.M.T., 1946
OLDHAM, Wilton, J., *The Hyphen in Rolls-Royce*, Foulis, 1967
PLOWDEN, William, *The Motor Car and Politics in Britain*, Pelican, 1973
RICARDO, Sir Harry, *Memories and Machines*, Constable, 1968
SHARP, Clifford, *The Problem of Transport*, Pergamon Press, 1965
TILLING, John, *Kings of the Highway*, Hutchinson, 1957
TURNER, Graham, *The Leyland Papers*, Eyre and Spottiswood, 1971
TWELVETREES and SQUIRE, *Why Dennis and How*, Guildford, 1945
WHITEHEAD, D., *Gardners of Patricroft*, Newman Neame, 1968
WISE, D. Burgess, *Veteran and Vintage Cars*, Hamlyn, 1970
The Times
The Commercial Motor

Appendix I

The Foden Range 1883–1975*

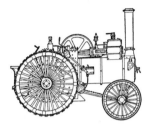

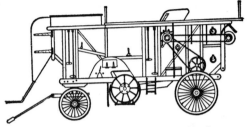

1. First traction engine 6 h.p. road locomotive manufactured 1883†

2. Thrashing machine exhaust and blast combined. This machine won the Society's prize medal at the Royal Agricultural Society's Show at York in 1883

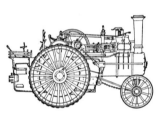

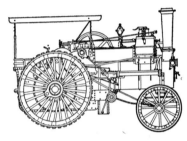

3. Double crank compound agricultural engine mounted on springs, 1890

4. Special road locomotive, 1890

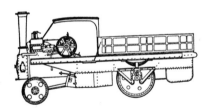

5. Prototype steam wagon manufactured in 1899

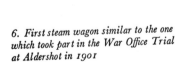

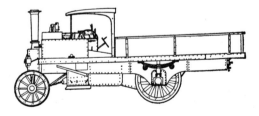

6. First steam wagon similar to the one which took part in the War Office Trial at Aldershot in 1901

* Where possible the drawings are to a common scale
† The year shown for each model is not necessarily the year of production of that model

173

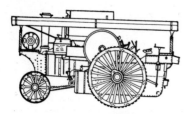

7. *Typical example of a travelling showman engine, 1902*

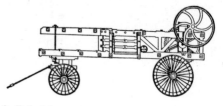

8. *Fodens' improved perpetual straw or hay baling press, 1902*

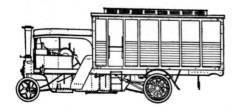

9. *5-ton steam wagon fitted with bus chassis, 1920*

10. *Flexible six-wheeler pantechnicon van cubic capacity of 1330 cubic feet, 1924*

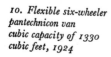

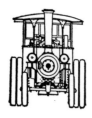

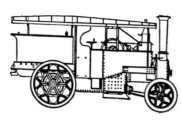

11. *Colonial steam tractor, 1924*

12. *6-ton steam wagon fitted with furniture removal van body, 1926*

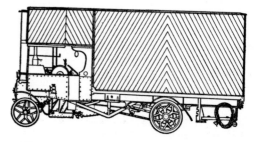

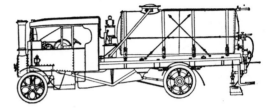

13. Overtype 12-ton six-wheel rigid steam wagon, 1926

14. 6-ton steam wagon fitted with tar spraying equipment, 1928

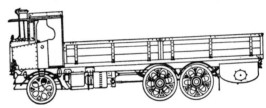

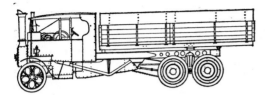

15. 6-ton E type steam wagon; this was the first undertype to be built, 1927

16. 12-ton E type six-wheel rigid eam wagon, 1928

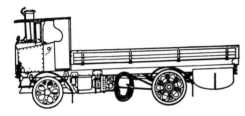

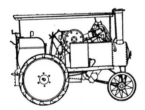

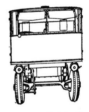

17. Agritractor 1920; this tractor was tted with an undertype engine

18. 1929 O type undertype four-wheel rigid

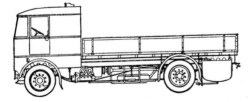

19. 'Speed Six' 6-ton undertype four-wheel rigid capable of speeds of up to sixty miles per hour, 1930

175

20. *'Speed twelve' 12-ton undertype. Capable of speeds of up to sixty miles per hour, 1930*

Both the 'Speed' type vehicles were fitted with pnuematic tyres and were the last steam vehicles to be developed at Fodens

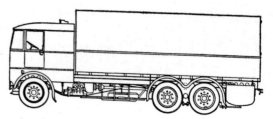

21. *No. 1 diesel fitted with Gardner engine, 1931*

22. *Foden type DG 6/7 7-ton diesel wagon fitted with 6 LW engine, 1932*

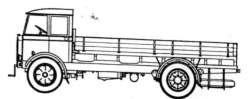

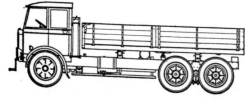

23. *Foden type DG 6/12 12-ton diesel wagon fitted with 16' three-way tipping body, 1932*

24. *Foden 2-ton diesel, 1934*

25. *S type 7-ton standard model fitted with 6 LW Gardner engine, 1935*

26. *S type 15½-ton load capacity and a platform length of 23' 8", 1935*

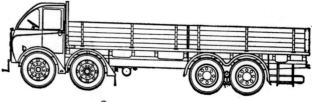

27. *Timber tractor fitted with a 5-cylinder Gardner engine in the transverse position, 1936*

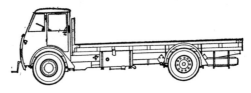

28. *Type OG4/4 four-wheel platform, 1937*

29. *Type DG 6/15 eight-wheel rigid platform 15-ton payload vehicle, 1938*

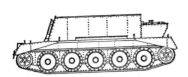

30. *Six-wheel army truck, over a thousand trucks were produced during World War II, 1939-45*

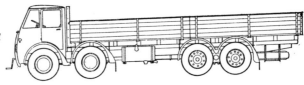

31. *Crusader, 17lb. anti-tank gun tower; six prototypes of this version of the Crusader were made at Fodens. Also a considerable number of Crusader battle tanks were manufactured during World War II*

32. *Centaur battle tank, 1940-5*

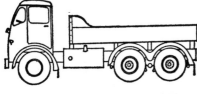

33. *Type FGHT 6/70 heavy duty independent tractor unit with S18 cab, 1948*

34. *Type FG 6/15 standard eight-wheel platform S18 cab, 1948*

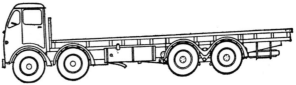

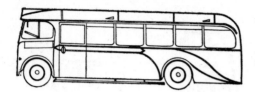

35. *Foden single-deck bus chassis 35-seater fitted with Gardner engine, 1948*

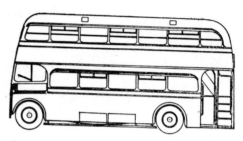

36. *Double-deck bus chassis 55-56-seater fitted with Gardner engine, 1949*

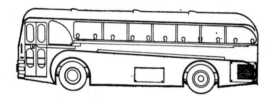

37. *Coach chassis fitted with Foden engine. Foden were the first to produce a rear engine bus, 1950*

38. *17-ton six-wheel twin steer platform vehicle fitted with S20 cab constructed of wood and aluminium, 1956*

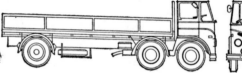

39. *Four-wheel tractor unit type FGTU 6/25 fitted with S21 fibreglass cab. This was the first fibreglass cab manufactured by Fodens, 1958*

40. *24-ton eight-wheeler fitted with S34 fibreglass tilt cab, 1962. The S34 fibreglass cab was the first British tilt cab on the market, 1962*

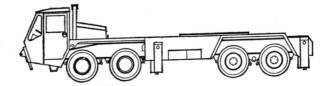

41. *Eight-wheel low line crane chassis. The first on the British market, 1963*

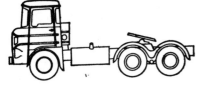

42. *100-ton heavy duty tractor unit fitted with S40 steel cab, 1967. This cab is still in production for export markets*

43. *30-ton gross eight-wheeler fitted with S39 fibreglass cab, 1972*

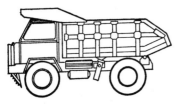

44. *Four-wheel dump truck FC17. The first four-wheel dump truck was introduced in 1954*

45. *Six-wheel dump truck FC27. This model is descended from the first Foden dump truck which was made in 1947 for the Steel Company of Wales*

46. *Six-wheel dump truck FC27A. This model is similar to the one above and is fitted with a semi-automatic gearbox, and was introduced in 1969*

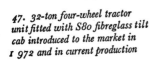

47. *32-ton four-wheel tractor unit fitted with S80 fibreglass tilt cab introduced to the market in 1972 and in current production*

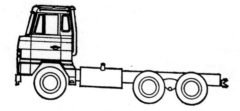

48. *26-ton rigid chassis left-hand drive fitted with S90 steel cab for the European market, introduced in 1974*

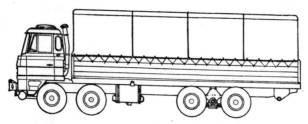
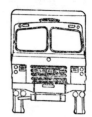

49. *Low mobility cargo army truck; over one thousand of these vehicles are on order for the British Army. This vehicle is fitted with S90 steel cab and is manufactured in right- and left-hand drive.*

50. *Medium mobility FH70 gun tractor. Developed for the British Army, this vehicle is an all-wheel drive or 4 × 2 drive cross-country vehicle*

51. *Four-wheel tractor unit, This vehicle is fitted in the 'Universal Range' of vehicles which was introduced in 1974 and will be in production in 1975. The vehicle is fitted with an S90 steel cab and will be available in right- and left-hand drive*

Appendix II

FIRST ORDERS FOR GARDNER LW ENGINES FROM MESSRS FODEN

Date	Quantity		
1931			
17 September	1	6LW/29267	Tested 30/10/31
1932			
29 February	3	6LW	
16 March	3	6LW	
30 March	1	6LW	
1 April	1	5LW	
1 April	6	6LW	
1 April	6	6LW	
16 April	12	6LW	
9 May	6	6LW	
21 June	12	6LW	
19 July	24	6LW	
29 July	1	4LW	
29 July	1	5LW	
27 September	1	5LW	
5 November	24	6LW	
7 November	1	4LW	
1933			
5 January	25	4LW	
17 January	1	5LW	
20 January	1	5LW	

FIRST ORDERS FOR GARDNER L2 ENGINES
FROM MESSRS FODEN

Date	Quantity		
1931			
20 February	1	5L2/28979	Tested 12/3/31
14 August	3	5L2	
14 August	3	6L2	
17 September	2	5L2	Cancelled
17 September	2	6L2	
24 September	12	6L2	
1932			
26 January	6	6L2	
29 February	3	6L2	Cancelled for 6LWs
16 March	3	6L2	Cancelled for 6LWs

Index